A BEGINNERS' GUIDE TO

2D SHOOTER GAMES WITH UNITY

Create a simple 2D shooter game and learn C# in the process

Patrick Felicia

A BEGINNER'S GUIDE TO

2D SHOOTER GAMES

WITH UNITY

First published: January 2017

Published by Patrick Felicia

CREDITS

Author: Patrick Felicia

ABOUT THE AUTHOR

Patrick Felicia is a <u>lecturer and researcher</u> at Waterford Institute of Technology, where he teaches and supervises undergraduate and postgraduate students. He obtained his MSc in Multimedia Technology in 2003 and PhD in Computer Science in 2009 from University College Cork, Ireland. He has published several books and articles on the use of video games for educational purposes, including the Handbook of Research on Improving Learning and Motivation through Educational Games: Multidisciplinary Approaches (published by IGI), and Digital Games in Schools: a Handbook for Teachers, published by European Schoolnet. Patrick is also the Editor-in-chief of the <u>International Journal of Game-Based Learning (IJGBL),</u> and the Conference Director of the <u>Irish Conference on Game-Based Learning</u>, a popular conference on games and learning organized throughout Ireland.

SUPPORT AND RESOURCES FOR THIS BOOK

To complete the activities presented in this book you need to download the startup pack on the companion website; it consists of free resources that you will need to complete your projects, including bonus material that will help you along the way (e.g., cheat sheets, introductory videos, code samples, and much more).

Please open the following link:

http://learntocreategames.com/2d-shooter-games/

In the section called "**Download your Free Resource Pack**", enter your email address and your first name, and click on the button labeled "**Yes, I want to receive my bonus pack**".

After a few seconds, you should receive a link to your free start-up pack.

When you receive the link, you can download all the resources to your computer.

This book is dedicated to Helena

TABLE OF CONTENTS

PREFACE

After teaching Unity for over 5 years, I always thought it could be great to find a book that could get my students started with Unity in a few hours and that showed them how to master the core functionalities offered by this fantastic software.

Many of the books that I found were too short and did not provide enough details on the why behind the actions recommended and taken; other books were highly theoretical, and I found that they lacked practicality and that they would not get my students' full attention. In addition, I often found that game development may be preferred by those with a programming background but that those with an Arts background, even if they wanted to get to know how to create games, often had to face the issue of learning to code for the first time.

As a result, I started to consider a format that would cover both: be approachable (even to the students with no programming background), keep students highly motivated and involved using an interesting project, cover the core functionalities available in Unity to get started with game programming, provide answers to common questions, and also provide, if need be, a considerable amount of details for some topics.

I then created a book series entitled **Unity From Zero to Proficiency** that did just this. It gave readers the opportunity to play around with Unity's core features, and essentially those that will make it possible to create an interesting 3D game rapidly. After reading this book series, many readers emailed me to let me know how the book series helped them; however, they also mentioned that what they also wanted was to be able to create a simple game from start to finish, publish it and share it with their friends.

This is the reason why I created this new book series entitled "**A Beginner's guide**"; it is targeted at people who already have completed the first four books in the series called **Unity From Zero to Proficiency**, and who would like to focus on a particular aspect of their game development. This being said, this new book series assumes no prior knowledge on the part of the reader, and it will get you started quickly on a particular aspect of Unity.

In this book, focused on 2D shooter games, you will be completing a 2D shooter game and also code in C#. By completing each chapter, and by following step-by-step instructions, you will progressively create a complete 2D shooter game.

You will also create a 2D game that includes many of the common techniques found in shooter games including: moving a spaceship, using moving targets, weapons, explosions, moving enemies, simple artificial intelligence, and a user interface.

CONTENT COVERED BY THIS BOOK

Chapter 1, *Creating a Simple Level*, shows you how to create a simple top-down level for a 2D shooter game, including: a spaceship that can be controlled, missiles, and targets that can be destroyed.

Chapter 2, *Adding Special Effects*, explains how it is possible to include visual effects that improve the quality of our game; you will learn how to make the targets blink when they are being hit, add explosions when NPCs are destroyed, and also include a scrolling background to give the impression of movement.

Chapter 3, *Improving Our Game*, explains how you can improve your game with simple but effective features including random events and artificial intelligence for NPCs that can fire missile at the player.

Chapter 4, *Polishing-up the Game,* shows how the game-play can be improved by progressively increasing the difficulty levels of the game over time (e.g., AI spawned more frequently) and also by making possible for the player to be temporary invincible with a shield.

Chapter 5 provides answers to Frequently Asked Questions (FAQs) related to the topics covered in this book.

Chapter 6 summarizes the topics covered in the book and provides you with more information on the next steps.

WHAT YOU NEED TO USE THIS BOOK

To complete the project presented in this book, you only need Unity 5.0 (or a more recent version) and to also ensure that your computer and its operating system comply with Unity's requirements. Unity can be downloaded from the official website (http://www.unity3d.com/download), and before downloading it, you can check that your computer is up to scratch on the following page: http://www.unity3d.com/unity/system-requirements. At the time of writing this book, the following operating systems are supported by Unity for development: Windows XP (i.e., SP2+, 7 SP1+), Windows 8, and Mac OS X 10.6+. In terms of graphics card, most cards produced after 2004 should be suitable.

In terms of computer skills, all knowledge introduced in this book will assume no prior programming experience from the reader. So for now, you only need to be able to perform common computer tasks, such as downloading items, opening and saving files, be comfortable with dragging and dropping items and typing, and be relatively comfortable with Unity's interface. This being said, because the focus of this book is on creating 2D platform games, and while all steps are explained step-by-step, you may need to be relatively comfortable with Unity's interface, and coding in C#, as well as creating and transforming objects.

So, if you would prefer to become more comfortable with Unity and C# programming prior to starting this book, you can download the books in the series called Unity 5 From Zero to Proficiency (Foundations, Beginner, or Intermediate, Advanced). These books cover most of the shortcuts and views available in Unity, as well as how to perform common tasks in Unity, such as creating objects, transforming objects, importing assets, using navigation controllers, creating scripts or exporting the game to the web. They also explain how to code your game using both UnityScript of C# along with good coding practices.

WHO THIS BOOK IS FOR

If you can answer **yes** to all these questions, then this book is for you:

1. Would you like to learn how to create a 2D shooter game?

2. Can you already code in C#?

3. Would you like to discover more 2D features in Unity?

4. Although you may have had some prior exposure to Unity and coding, would you like to delve more into 2D shooter games?

WHO THIS BOOK IS NOT FOR

If you can answer yes to all these questions, then this book is **not** for you:

1. Can you already create 2D shooter games?

2. Are you looking for a reference book on Unity programming?

3. Are you an experienced (or at least advanced) Unity user?

If you can answer yes to all four questions, you may instead look for the next book series on the <u>official website</u>.

HOW YOU WILL LEARN FROM THIS BOOK

Because all students learn differently and have different expectations of a course, this book is designed to ensure that all readers find a learning mode that suits them. Therefore, it includes the following:

- A list of the learning objectives at the start of each chapter so that readers have a snapshot of the skills that will be covered.

- Each section includes an overview of the activities covered.

- Many of the activities are step-by-step, and learners are also given the opportunity to engage in deeper learning and problem-solving skills through the challenges offered at the end of each chapter.

- Each chapter ends-up with a quiz and challenges through which you can put your skills (and knowledge acquired) into practice, and see how much you know. Challenges consist in coding, debugging, or creating new features based on the knowledge that you have acquired in the chapter.

- The book focuses on the core skills that you need; some sections also go into more detail; however, once concepts have been explained, links are provided to additional resources, where necessary.

- The code is introduced progressively and is explained in detail.

- You also gain access to several videos that help you along the way, especially for the most challenging topics.

FORMAT OF EACH CHAPTER AND WRITING CONVENTIONS

Throughout this book, and to make reading and learning easier, text formatting and icons will be used to highlight parts of the information provided and to make it more readable.

The full solution for the project presented in this book is available for download on the official website (http://learntocreategames.com/2d-shooter-games/).

SPECIAL NOTES

Each chapter includes resource sections, so that you can further your understanding and mastery of Unity; these include:

- A quiz for each chapter: these quizzes usually include 10 questions that test your knowledge of the topics covered throughout the chapter. The solutions are provided on the companion website.

- A checklist: it consists of between 5 and 10 key concepts and skills that you need to be comfortable with before progressing to the next chapter.

- Challenges: each chapter includes a challenge section where you are asked to combine your skills to solve a particular problem.

Author's notes appear as described below:

Author's suggestions appear in this box.

Code appears as described below:

```
public int score;
public string playersName = "Sam";
```

Checklists that include the important points covered in the chapter appear as described below:

- Item1 for check list
- Item2 for check list
- Item3 for check list

HOW CAN YOU LEARN BEST FROM THIS BOOK?

- **Talk to your friends about what you are doing.**

  We often think that we understand a topic until we have to explain it to friends and answer their questions. By explaining your different projects, what you just learned will become clearer to you.

- **Do the exercises.**

  All chapters include exercises that will help you to learn by doing. In other words, by completing these exercises, you will be able to better understand the topic and gain practical skills (i.e., rather than just reading).

- **Don't be afraid of making mistakes.**

  I usually tell my students that making mistakes is part of the learning process; the more mistakes you make and the more opportunities you have for learning. At the start, you may find the errors disconcerting, or that the engine does not work as expected until you understand what went wrong.

- **Export your games early.**

  It is always great to build and export your first game. Even if it is rather simple, it is always good to see it in a browser and to be able to share it with you friends.

- **Learn in chunks.**

  It may be disconcerting to go through five or six chapters straight, as it may lower your motivation. Instead, give yourself enough time to learn, go at your own pace, and learn in small units (e.g., between 15 and 20 minutes per day). This will do at least two things for you: it will give your brain the time to "digest" the information that you have just learned, so that you can start fresh the following day. It will also make sure that you don't "burn-out" and that you keep your motivation levels high.

FEEDBACK

While I have done everything possible to produce a book of high quality and value, I always appreciate feedback from readers so that the book can be improved accordingly. If you would like to give feedback, you can email me at learntocreategames@gmail.com.

DOWNLOADING THE SOLUTIONS FOR THE BOOK

You can download the solutions for this book after creating a free online account at http://learntocreategames.com/2d-shooter-games/. Once you have registered, a link to the files will be sent to you automatically.

IMPROVING THE BOOK

Although great care was taken in checking the content of this book, I am human, and some errors could remain in the book. As a result, it would be great if you could let me know of any issue or error you may have come across in this book, so that it can be solved and the book updated accordingly. To report an error, you can email me (learntocreategames@gmail.com) with the following information:

- Name of the book.

- The page or section where the error was detected.

- Describe the error and also what you think the correction should be.

Once your email is received, the error will be checked, and, in the case of a valid error, it will be corrected and the book page will be updated to reflect the changes accordingly.

SUPPORTING THE AUTHOR

A lot of work has gone into this book and it is the fruit of long hours of preparation, brainstorming, and finally writing. As a result, I would ask that you do not distribute any illegal copies of this book.

This means that if a friend wants a copy of this book, s/he will have to buy it through the official channels (i.e., through Amazon, lulu.com, or the book's official website: www.learntocreategames.com/learn-unity-ebook).

If some of your friends are interested in the book, you can refer them to the book's official website (http://www.learntocreategames.com/learn-unity-ebook) where they can either buy the book, enter a monthly draw to be in for a chance of receiving a free copy of the book, or to be notified of future promotional offers.

1

CREATING A SIMPLE LEVEL

In this section, we will start by creating a simple level, including:

- A spaceship symbolized by a triangle that you will be able to move in four directions.

- The ability for the spaceship to fire missiles.

- The ability for the player to destroy targets with the missiles.

- A camera that displays the scene.

- Meteorites (or moving targets) generated randomly.

So, after completing this chapter, you will be able to:

- Detect keystrokes.

- Generate random events.

- Instantiate objects.

- Add velocity to objects (i.e., to the moving targets).

- Modify sprites' properties such as their color.

- Move objects from a script.

ADDING THE SPACESHIP

So, in this section, we will start to create the spaceship that will be used by the player; it will consist of a simple sprite (for the time-being) that we will be able to move in four directions using the arrow keys on the keyboard: left, right, up and down.

So, let's get started:

- Please launch Unity and create a new Project (**File | New Project**).

Figure 1: Creating a new project

- In the new window, you can specify the name of your project, its location, as well as the **2D** mode (as this game will be **2D**).

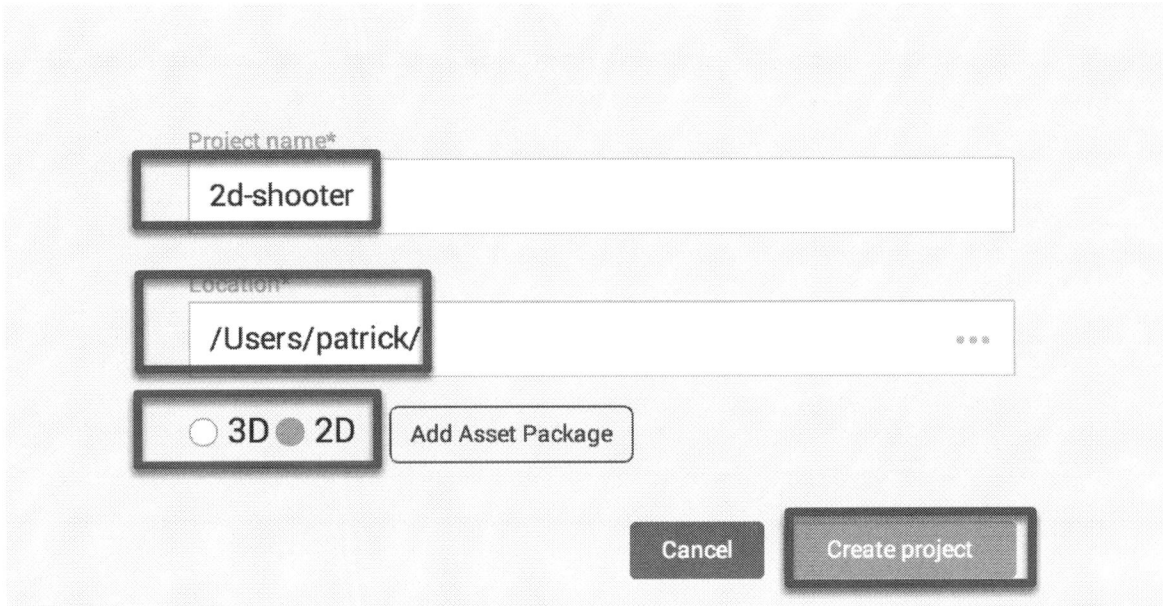

Figure 2: Specifying the name and location for your project

- Once this is done, you can click on the button called **Create project** (at the bottom of the window) and Unity should open.

- Once this is done, you can check that the 2D mode is activated, based on the 2D logo located in the top right-corner of the **Scene** view.

Figure 3: Activating the 2D mode

We will now create a new sprite for our spaceship; it will be made of a simple triangle.

- From the **Project** view, please select **Create | Sprites | Triangle**, as illustrated on the next figure.

Figure 4: Creating a new sprite

- This will create a new asset called **Triangle** in the **Project** window.

Figure 5: Creating a new triangle asset

- Once this is done, you can drag and drop this sprite (i.e., the white object with the label **Triangle**) from the **Project** window to the **Scene** view; this will create a new object called **Triangle** in the **Hierarchy** view.

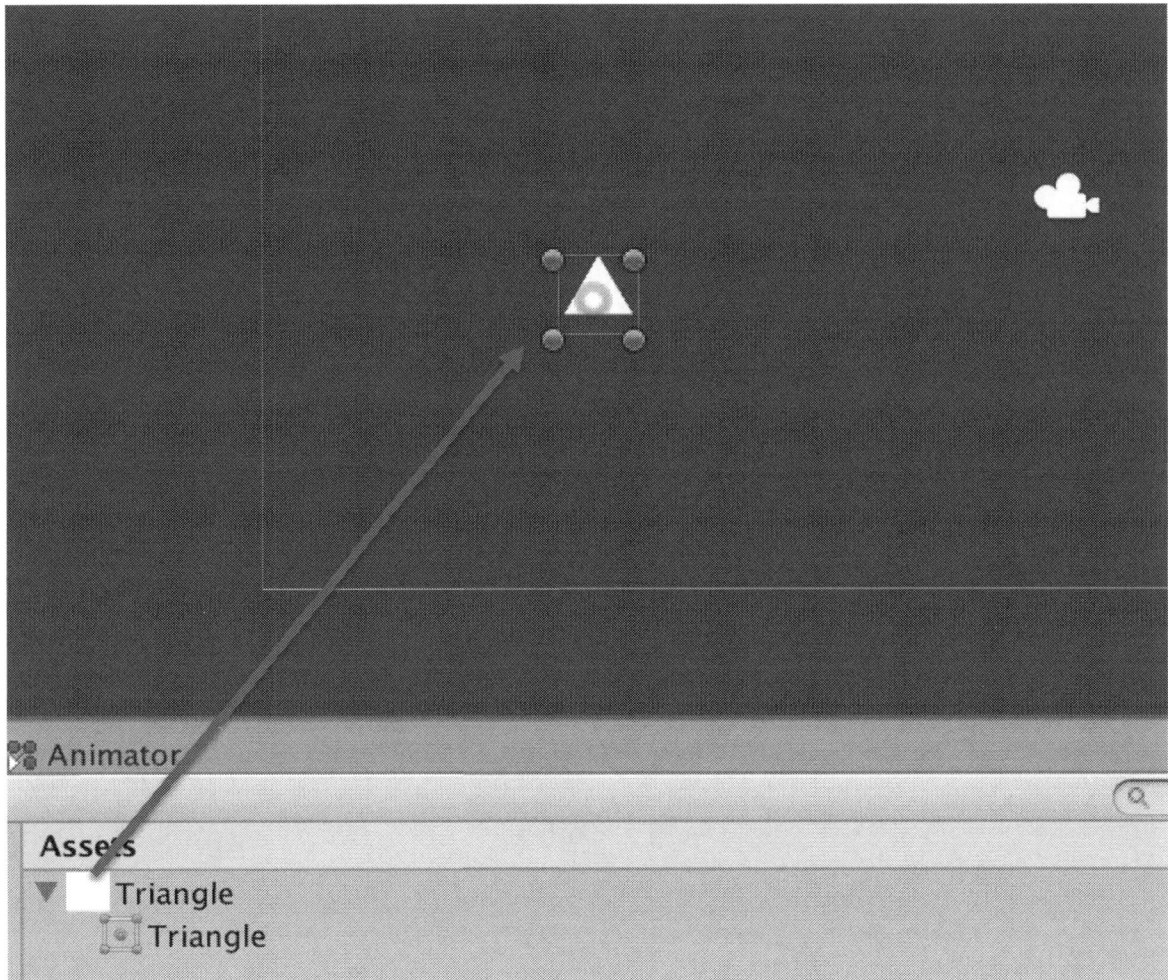

Figure 6: adding the player character

In the previous window, you may notice the white lines at the bottom and to the left of the screen; these are the boundaries that define what will be visible onscreen; so by dropping your object within these lines, you ensure that the player will be seen (or captured) by the camera.

- Please rename this object **player** for now, using the **Hierarchy** window: to rename this object, you can right-click on it in the **Hierarchy** window, and then select the option **Rename** from the contextual menu.

So at this stage, we have a new player character (i.e., the spaceship) and we will need to move it according to the keys pressed on the keyboard; so let's do just this:

- Please create a new C# script (i.e., select **Create | C# Script** from the **Project** window) and rename this script **MovePlayer**.

- Once this is done, please open this script and add the following code to it (new code in bold):

```
void Update ()
{
    if (Input.GetKey (KeyCode.LeftArrow))
    {
        gameObject.transform.Translate (Vector3.left * 0.1f);
    }
    if (Input.GetKey (KeyCode.RightArrow))
    {
        gameObject.transform.Translate (Vector3.right * 0.1f);
    }
    if (Input.GetKey (KeyCode.UpArrow))
    {
        gameObject.transform.Translate (Vector3.up * 0.1f);
    }
    if (Input.GetKey (KeyCode.DownArrow))
    {
        gameObject.transform.Translate (Vector3.down * 0.1f);
    }

}
```

In the previous code:

- We use the function **Update** to check for keyboard inputs.

- If the **left** arrow is pressed, we move the object linked to this script (i.e., the spaceship) to the **left** (i.e., 0.1 meter to the left).

- If the **right** arrow is pressed, we move the object linked to this script (i.e., the spaceship) to the **right** (i.e., 0.1 meter to the right).

Note that we use the function **GetKey** that checks whether a key has been pressed; however, if you wanted to check whether a key has been released then you could use the function **GetKeyDown** instead.

You can now save the script, check for any error in the **Console** window, and link the script (i.e., drag and drop it) to the object called **player** that is in the **Hierarchy** view. Once this is done, you can play the scene and check that you can move the player left or right. After pressing the arrow keys on your keyboard, you should see that the spaceship moves in four directions.

Note that to play and stop the scene, you can press the shortcut **CTRL + P**, or use the black triangle located at the top of the window.

SHOOTING MISSILES

In this section, we will get the player to shoot missiles whenever s/he presses the space bar; this will involve the following steps:

- Creating an object for the missile.

- Saving this object as a prefab (i.e., a template).

- Detecting when the space bar has been pressed (and then released) by the player.

- Instantiating the missile prefab and adding velocity to it so that it moves up when fired.

First, let's create a new object for the missile:

- You can now stop the scene (e.g., CTRL + P).

- Using the **Project** window, please create a new circular sprite (**Create | Sprites | Circle**), and rename it **bullet**.

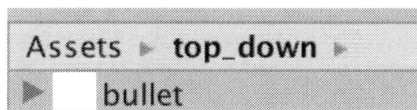

Assets ▸ top_down ▸
▸ bullet

Figure 7: Creating a bullet

- Once this is done, please drag and drop this **bullet** asset from the **Project** window to the **Scene** (or **Hierarchy**) window, this will create a new object called **bullet**.

- Using the **Inspector**, rescale this object to **(0.1, 0.1, 0.1)**. The position of this object does not matter for now.

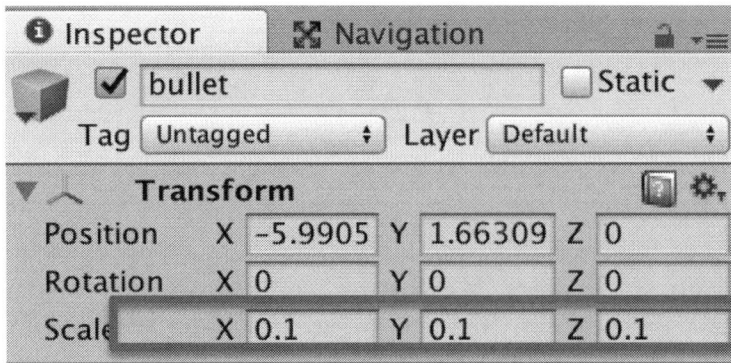

Figure 8: Scaling-down the bullet

- Add a **Rigidbody2D** component to this object (i.e., select **Components | Physics2D | Rigidbody2D** from the top menu) and set the **Gravity Scale** attribute of this component (i.e., **Rigidbody2D**) to **0,** as illustrated in the next figure.

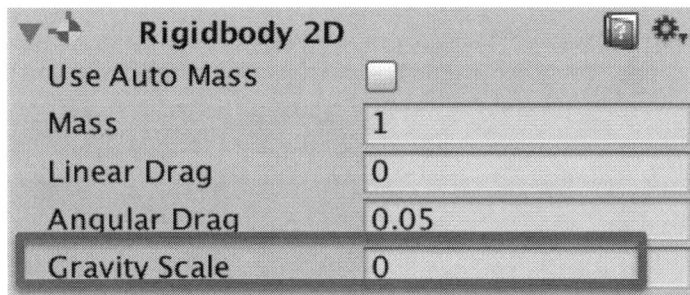

Figure 9: Setting the gravity scale

By adding a **Rigidbody2D** component to this object, we ensure that we can apply forces to it, or modify its velocity; this being said, because we have a top-down view, we do not want this object to be influenced by gravity (otherwise it would fall down), and this is why we set the **Gravity Scale** attribute to **0** for this object.

- We can now convert this **bullet** to a prefab by dragging and dropping this object (i.e., **bullet**) to the **Project** view.

Figure 10: Creating a prefab for the bullet

- You can now delete the object called **bullet** from the **Hierarchy**.

Last but not least, we need to add some code that will be used to instantiate and propel this bullet if the player presses the space bar.

- Please open the script called **MovePlayer**.

- Add the following code at the beginning of the script (new code in bold).

```
public class MovePlayer : MonoBehaviour
{
    public GameObject bullet;
```

- Please add the following code to the **Update** function:

```
if (Input.GetKeyDown (KeyCode.Space))
{
    GameObject   b   =   (GameObject)(Instantiate  (bullet,
transform.position + transform.up*1.5f, Quaternion.identity));
        b.GetComponent<Rigidbody2D>  ().AddForce  (transform.up  *
1000);
}
```

In the previous code:

- We create a new **GameObject**.

- This **GameObject** will be based on the template called **bullet**.

- If the player hits the space bar, the new bullet is instantiated just above the spaceship.

- We then add an upward force to the bullet so that it starts to move.

You can now save your script, and check that it is error-free in the **Console** window.

- If you click on the object called **player** that is present in the **Hierarchy**, and if you look at the **Inspector**, you should see that a new field called **bullet** has appeared for the component **MovePlayer**.

- Please drag and drop the prefab called **bullet** to this field (as illustrated on the next figure).

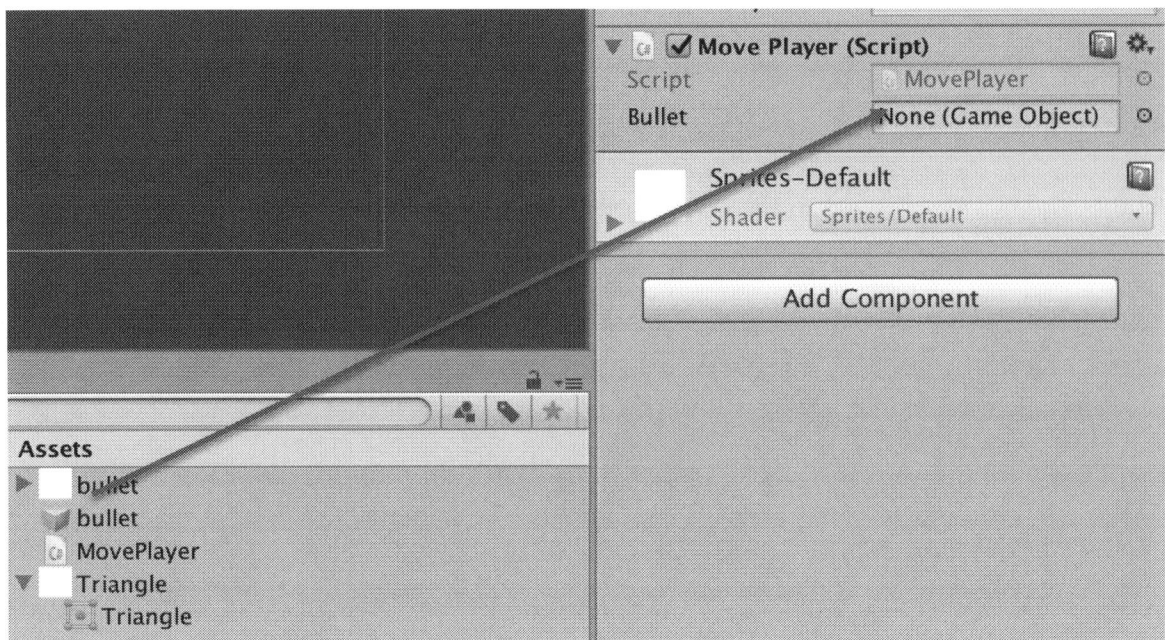

Figure 11:Adding the bullet prefab

Once this done, you can play the scene, and check that after pressing the space bar, you are able to fire a bullet.

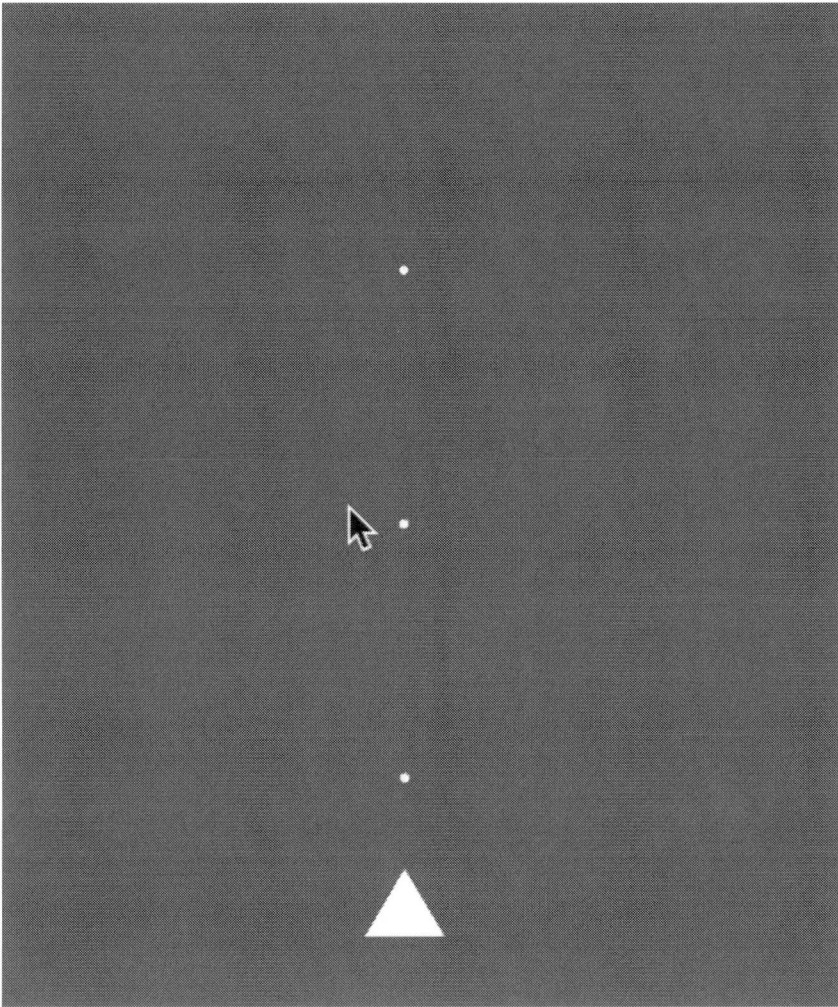

Figure 12: Shooting projectiles

DESTROYING THE TARGET

Now that we can shoot missiles (or bullets), we just need to be able to destroy the objects colliding with the missiles; so we will create new objects that will be used as targets for the time being.

- Please create a new **Square** sprite (from the **Project** window, select: **Create Sprites | Square**) or you can also duplicate the **player** sprite if you wish.

- Rename this new sprite **target**.

- Drag and drop this sprite to the **Scene** view.

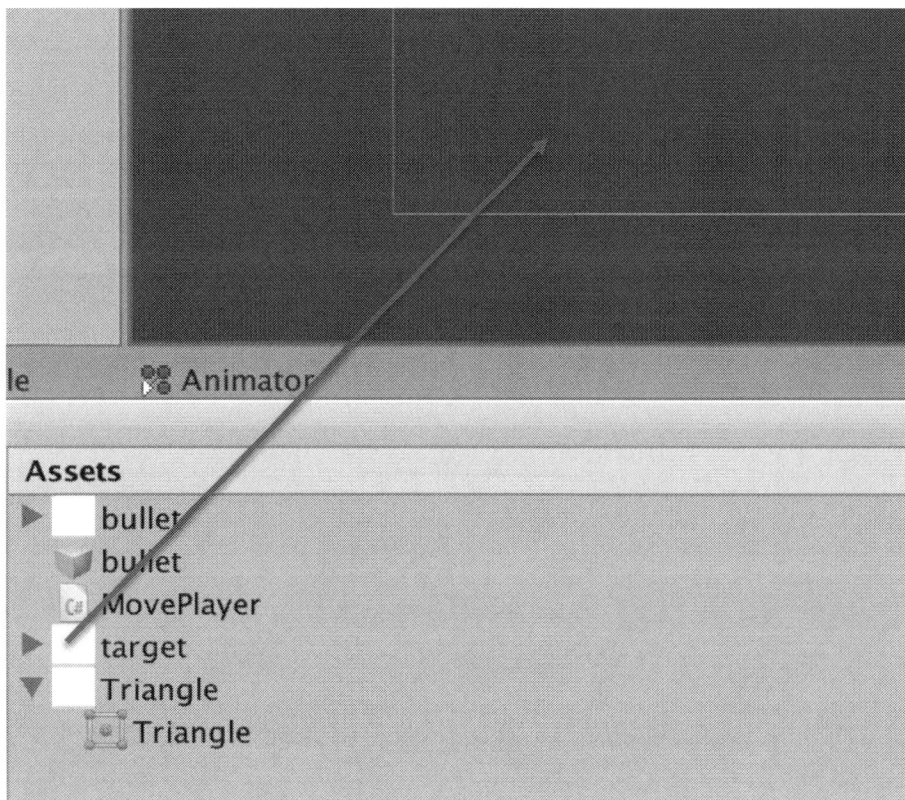

Figure 13: Adding a target to the scene

- This will create a new object; rename this new object **target**.

- Please select this object.

Add a **BoxCollider2D** to this object (i.e., select **Components | Physics2D | BoxCollider2D** from the top menu). This is so that collisions can be detected.

We will now create a new tag for this object. A **tag**; will help to identify each object in the scene, and to see the object that the bullets (or the player) are colliding with.

- Please select the object called **target** in the **Hierarchy**.

- In the **Inspector** window, click on the drop-down menu called **Untagged** (to the right of the attribute called tag), as described on the next figure.

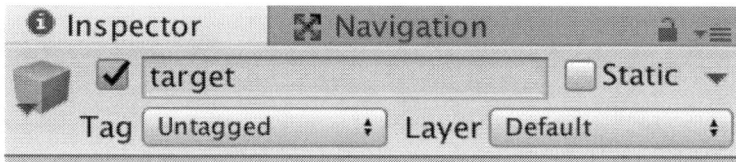

Figure 14: Creating a tag (part1)

- From the drop-down menu, please select the option **Add Tag...**

Figure 15: Creating a tag (part 2)

- In the new window, click on the + button that is located below the label "**Tags/List is Empty**".

Figure 16: Creating a tag (part 3)

- Please specify a name for your tag (i.e., **target**), using the field to the right of the label **Tag 0**.

Figure 17: Adding a tag (part 2)

- Press the **Enter/Return** key on your keyboard to save your new tag.

- Select the object **target** in the **Hierarchy** again, and, using the **Inspector**, select the tag **target**, that you have just created.

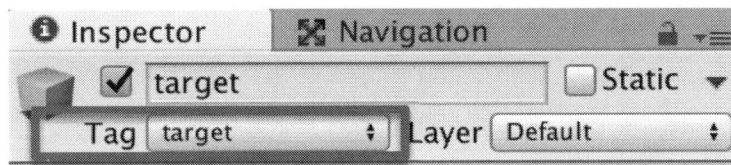

Figure 18: Adding a tag (part 3)

- Last but not least, we will create a prefab from this target by dragging and dropping the object **target** to the **Project** window.

Next, we will create a new script that will be linked to the bullet (or missile), so that, upon collision with a target, this target should be destroyed (based on its tag).

- Please create a new script called **Bullet**: from the **Project** window, select **Create | C# Script**.

- Open this script.

- Add the following code to it (just **after** the function **Update**).

```
void OnCollisionEnter2D(Collision2D coll)
{
    if (coll.gameObject.tag == "target")
    {
        Destroy (coll.gameObject);
        Destroy (gameObject);
    }
}
```

In the previous code:

- We detect the objects colliding with the bullet.

- When this occurs, we check if this object is a target; if this is the case, this target is then destroyed.

- The bullet is also destroyed in this case.

Once this is done, we can save our script and link it to the **bullet** prefab.

- Please save the script called **Bullet** and check that it is error-free.

- Once this is done, please drag and drop it on the prefab called **Bullet**, in the **Project** window.

- You can then click once on the prefab called **bullet**, and check, using the **Inspector** window, that it includes the script **Bullet**.

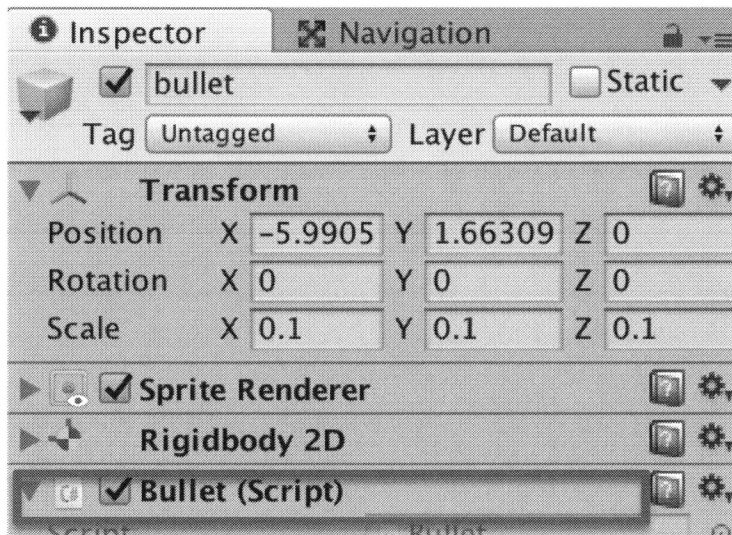

Figure 19: Checking the components of the Bullet prefab

Last but not least, we will need to add a collider to our **Bullet** prefab, so that it actually collides with other objects:

- Please select the prefab called **bullet**.

- From the top menu, select **Components | Physics2D | BoxCollider2D**.

You can now test your game:

- Move the target object just above the **player**, as illustrated in the next figure.

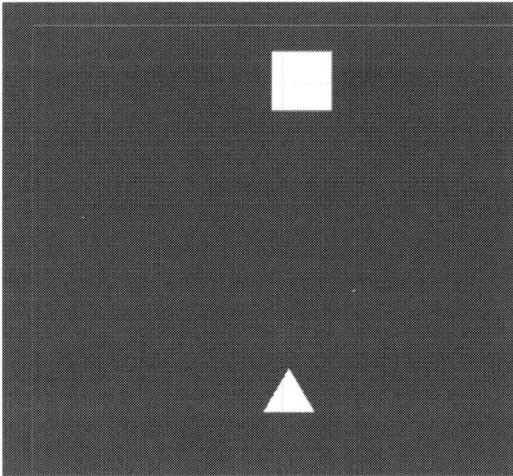

Figure 20: Checking the bullet prefab

- Please play the scene, fire a missile (i.e., press the space bar), and check that, upon collision between the bullet and the target, both objects are destroyed.

> Note that since you will be firing several bullets, we could choose to destroy a bullet after 10 seconds (by this time it should have hit a target), by modifying the script **Bullet** as follows (new code in bold):

```
void Start ()
{
    Destroy (gameObject, 10);
}
```

You can test your scene and see that after 10 seconds the bullet is destroyed.

Before we go ahead, it may be a good idea to save our scene:

- Please select **File | Save Scene As** from the top menu, and save your scene as **level1**.

- You can also save your project (**File | Save Project**).

Next, we will just create a slightly different type of target; that is: a moving target that will move downwards and that the player will have to avoid or to destroy; so let's implement this feature:

- Using the **Project** window, please duplicate the prefab called **target**, that we have just created (i.e., select the **target** prefab, and the press *CTRL + D*).

- Rename the duplicate **moving_target** (i.e., right-click + **Rename**).

- Select the prefab **moving_target** in the **Hierarchy** and add a RigidBody2D component to it (i.e., select **Component | Physics2D | RigidBody2D**).

- Using the Inspector window, set its attribute called **Gravity Scale** (for the component **Rigidbody2D**) to 0, as illustrated on the next figure. This is so that the object does not fall indefinitely (since it is a top-down view).

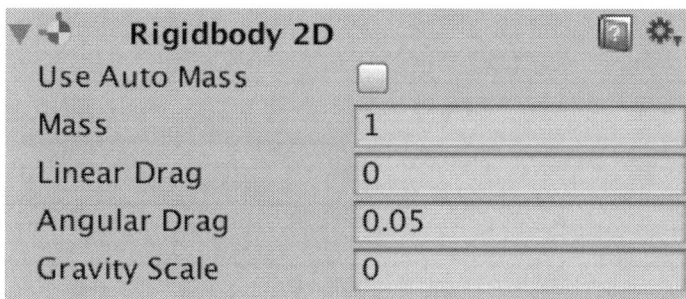

Figure 21: Adjusting the gravity scale

Next, we will create a script that will be linked to this object and that will set its initial velocity downwards.

- Please create a new C# script called **MovingTarget**.

- Modify the **Start** function as follows (new code in bold).

```
void Start ()
{
    GetComponent<Rigidbody2D> ().velocity = Vector2.down * 10;
}
```

In the previous code, we access the **Rigidbody2D** component of the object linked to this script (this will be the moving target), and then set the velocity downwards.

- You can now save your script, check that it is error-free, and drag and drop it to the prefab called **moving_target**.

Figure 22: Linking the script to the target

- So that we can test the scene, please drag and drop the prefab **moving_target** to the **Scene** view and play the scene, you should see that this particular target moves downwards.

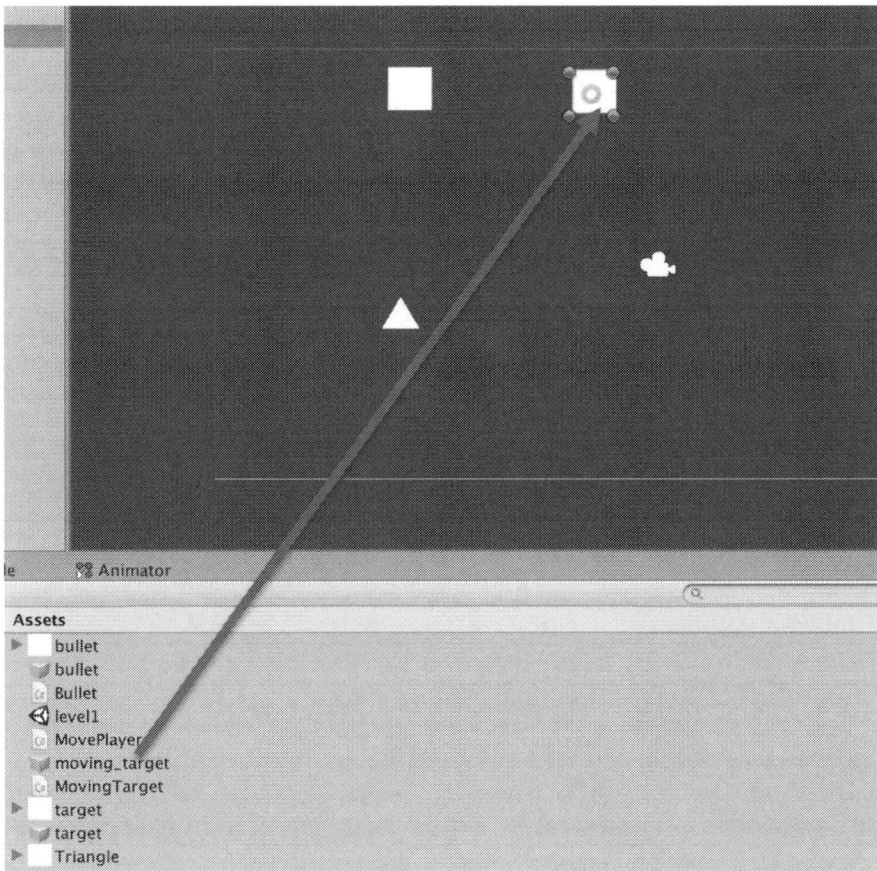

Figure 23: Adding a moving target to the scene

SPAWNING MOVING TARGETS RANDOMLY

Last but not least, we will create a mechanism through which the moving targets are created randomly, a bit like meteorites, so that flying "meteorites" appear randomly onscreen and move downwards. For this, we will be doing the following:

- We will create an empty object that will spawn these moving targets.

- These will be instantiated at regular intervals and at random positions.

- We will also ensure that the moving targets are spawned in the current view (i.e., relatively close to the player so that they can be captured and displayed by the camera).

So let's get to it:

- Please create a new empty object called **targetSpawner** in the **Hierarchy** window (i.e., select **GameObject | Create Empty**).

- Create a new C# script called **SpawnMovingTargets**.

- Open the script.

- Add the following code at the beginning of the class (new code in bold):

```
public class SpawnMovingTargets : MonoBehaviour {
float timer = 0;
public GameObject newObject;
```

- Add the following code to the **Update** function (new code in bold):

```
void Update ()
{
    timer += Time.deltaTime;
    float range = Random.Range (-10, 10);
    Vector3        newPosition        =        new        Vector3
(GameObject.Find("player").transform.position.x        +        range,
transform.position.y, 0);
    if (timer >= 1)
    {
        GameObject  t  =  (GameObject)(Instantiate  (newObject,
newPosition, Quaternion.identity));
        timer = 0;
    }
}
```

In the previous code:

- We increase the value of our timer every seconds.

- We then define a variable called **range**; it will be a random number between **-10** and **10**; this variable will be used to define a random position that is to the left (i.e., **-10 to 0**) or to the right (i.e., **0 to +10**) of the player; this is so that the target instantiated is close enough to the player and within the field of the view of the camera.

- We then create a new vector called **newPosition** that uses the variable **range** defined earlier for the **x coordinate;** the **y-coordinate** of the object linked to this script (this will be the empty object **targetSpawner**) is then used for the **y-coordinate** of the object that is being instantiated.

- A new object is then instantiated every second: every time the value of the variable **timer** is greater than 1, **timer** is reset to 0 and a new prefab (i.e., moving target) is instantiated

There are of course many other ways to create this feature, but this version is relatively simple, to start with.

Next, we just need to set-up the **targetSpawner** object:

- Please check that the script that you have just created is error-free.

- Drag and drop this script (i.e., **SpawnMovingTargets**) to the object called **targetSpawner** in the **Hierarchy**. Alternatively, you can add the script to the object **targetSpawner** by selecting this object in the **Hierarhcy**, and by then dragging and dropping the script (i.e., **SpawnMovingTargets**) to the **Inspector** window, as illustrated on the next figure.

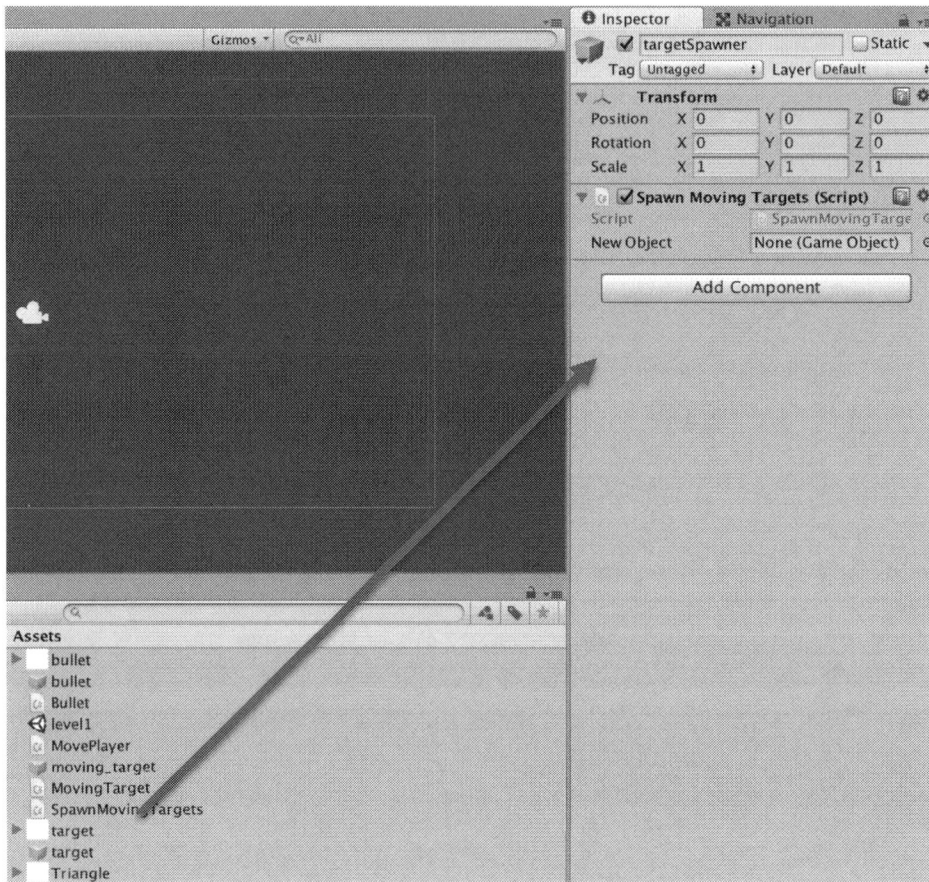

Figure 24: Adding a script to the object targetSpawner

- Please select the object **targetSpawner** in the **Hierarchy** window.

- Drag the prefab called **moving_target** from the **Project** window to the field called **newObject** in the **Inspector**, as described in the next figure.

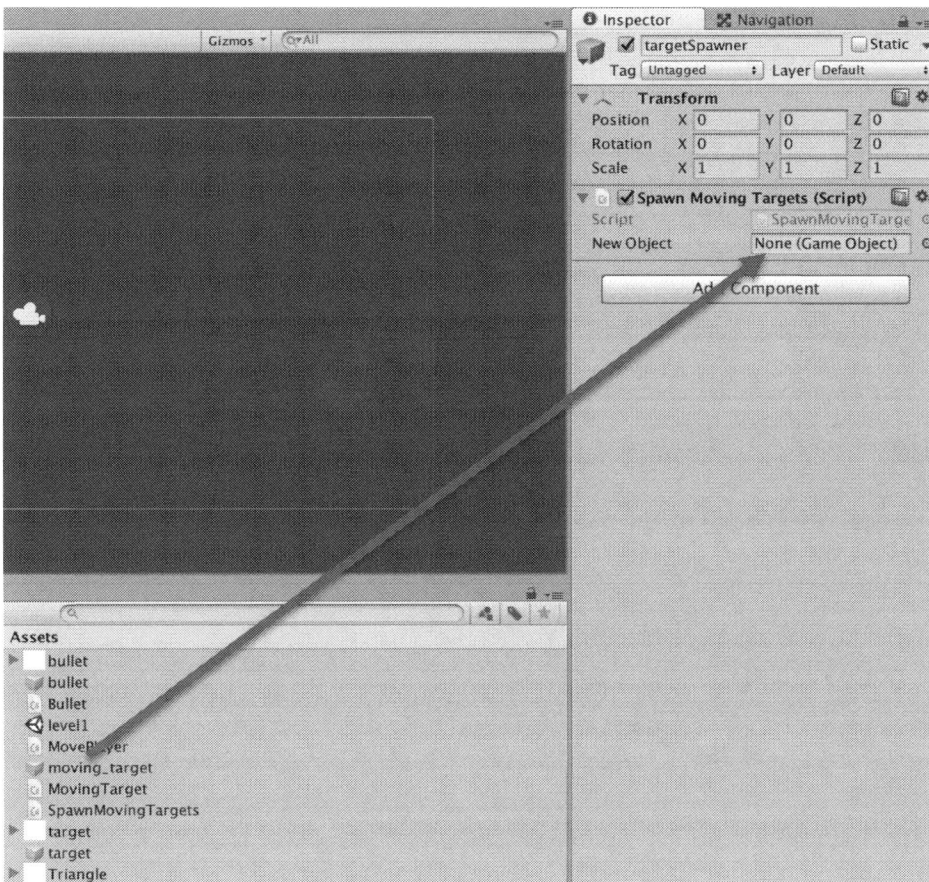

Figure 25: Setting the prefab to be spawn (part 1)

- The component **SawnMovingTarget** should then look as follows.

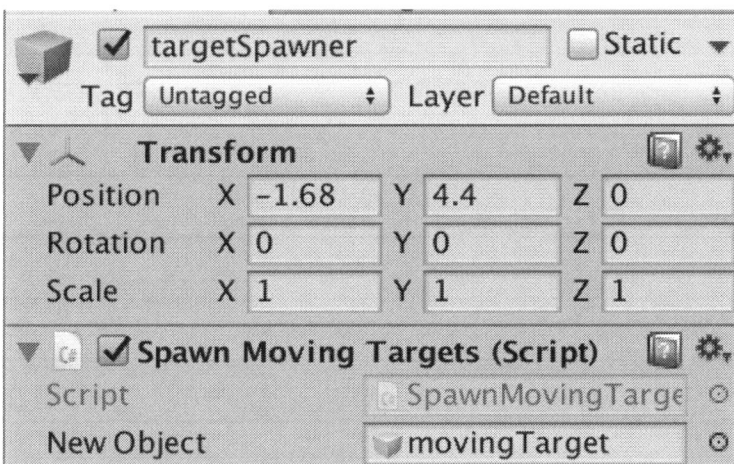

Figure 26: Setting the prefab to be spawn (part 2)

Last, using the **Scene** view, we just need to move the object called **targetSpawner** at the upper boundary of the screen; this is so that the moving targets are instantiated at the very top of the screen, just above the player.

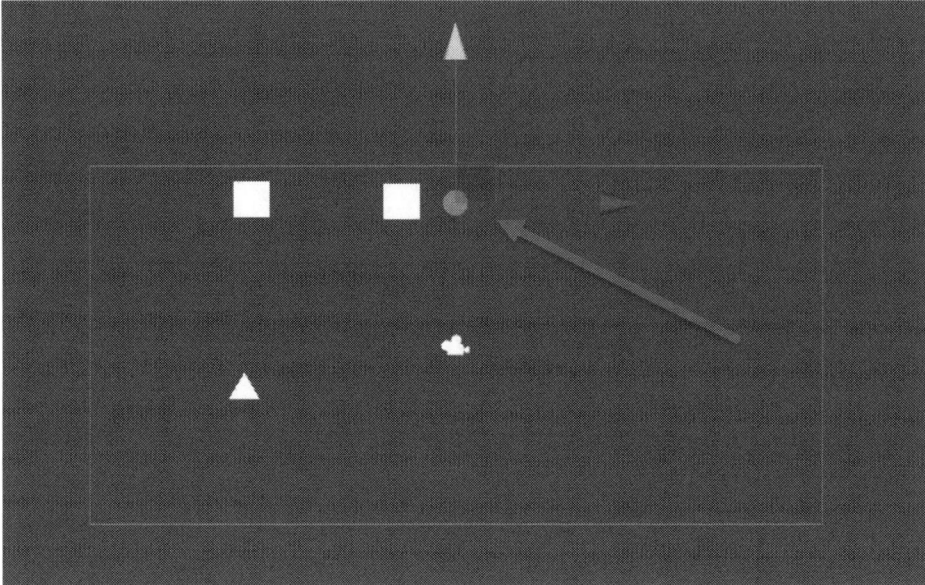

Figure 27: Moving the targetSpawner object

Once this is done, you can delete or deactivate the objects called **moving_target** and **target** that are already in the scene (i.e., the two squares that you could see in the previous figure), and test the scene. To deactivate these objects, you can select them and, using the **Inspector** window, uncheck the box to the left of their name.

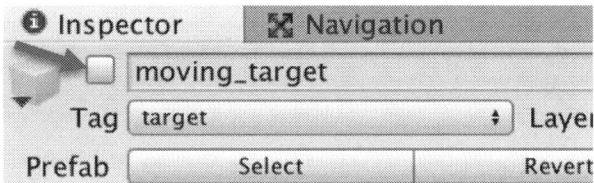

Figure 28: Deactivating the moving target

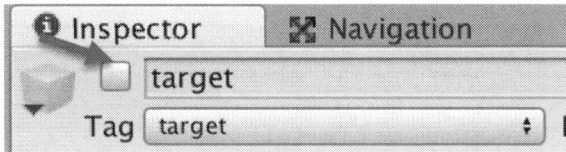

Figure 29: Deactivating the target

As you play the scene, you should see that a new moving target is instantiated every second at random, as described on the next figure.

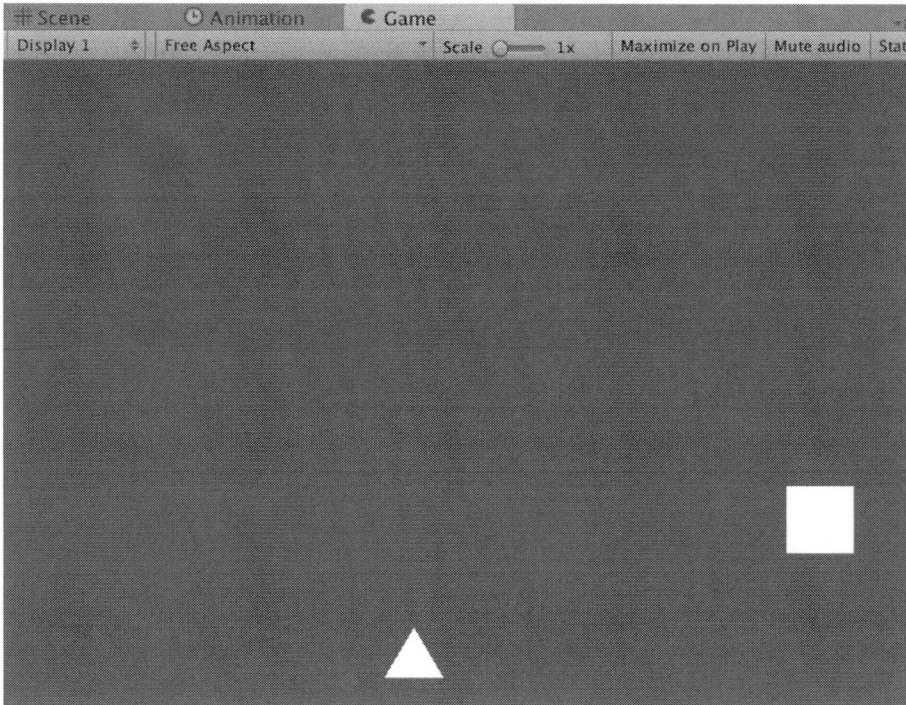

Figure 30: Spawning moving targets

MANAGING DAMAGE

Now that we have created a moving target that the player can shoot, we will create a script that manages the damage taken by the target so that it is destroyed only after being hit several times by the player's bullets.

- Please create a new script called **ManageTargetHealth** (i.e., select **Create | C# Script** from the **Project** window)

- Add the following code at the beginning of the class (new code in bold).

```
public class ManageTargetHealth : MonoBehaviour {
    public int health, type;
    public static int TARGET_BOULDER = 0;
```

- In the previous code, we create three variables: **health**, **type**, and **TARGET_BOULDER**.

- **health** will be used to determine the health (or strength) of each target so that we know how much damage it can sustain before being destroyed.

- **type** is used to set different types of targets; each of these will have different levels of health (or strength).

- **TARGET_BOULDER** will be used as a type for our moving targets (i.e., boulders). Note that this variable is both **static** and **public**; this means that it can be accessed from outside its class; also, because it is **static**, this variable can be accessed without the need to instantiate a new object of type **ManageTargetHealth**.

> We will come back to this principle later, but in a nutshell, static variables and functions can be used by other classes with no instantiation required; you can consider these static variables and functions as utility classes and variables that can be used without the need to be part of a particular class, a bit like a friend granting your access to his or her car without the need for you to be the owner. For example, the function **Debug.Log** can be used from anywhere in your game, although, you don't need to instantiate an object of type **Debug** for this purpose; the same holds true for the function **GameObject.Find**; again, you can use this function to find a particular object; however, you don't need to instantiate an object of class **GameOBject** to be able to use this function **Find**.

Now, we just need to specify the health (or strength) of the target, based on its type, in the **Start** function.

- Please add the following code to the **Start** function (new code in bold).

```
void Start ()
{
    if (type == TARGET_BOULDER) health = 20;
}
```

- Add a new function called **gotHit**, at the end of the class (i.e., before the last closing curly bracket) as follows:

```
public void gotHit(int dammage)
{
    health-= dammage;
    if (health <= 0)
    destroyTarget ();
}
```

In the previous code:

- We declare a function called **gotHit**; its return type is **void** because it does not return any value; it takes a parameter of type **int** that will be referred to as **damage** within this function.

- We then set the value of the variable **health** by subtracting the value of the variable **damage** from the previous value of the variable **health**; this is equivalent to the following code:

```
health = health - damage;
```

- If the **health** is **0** or less, we then call the function called **destroyTarget**.

We now just need to create the function called **destroyTarget**.

- Please add a new function called **destroyTarget** at the end of the class (i.e., before the last closing curly bracket) as follows:

```
public void destroyTarget()
{
    Destroy (gameObject);
}
```

In the previous code:

- We create a new function called **destroyTarget** of type **void** (since it does not return any value).

- This function destroys the object linked to this script (i.e., the target).

Once this is done, we can save and use this script:

- Please save your code and check that it is error-free.

- Using the **Project** view, drag and drop this script (i.e., **ManageTargetHealth)** on both the **target** and the **moving_target** prefabs.

Next, we just need to modify the script **SpawnMovingTarget** so that we specify the type of the target that is to be created.

- Please modify the spawning script (i.e., **SpawnMovingTargets**) as follows (new code in bold).

```
if (timer >= 1)
{
    GameObject    t    =    (GameObject)(Instantiate    (newObject,
newPosition, Quaternion.identity));
    t.GetComponent<ManageTargetHealth>             ().type           =
ManageTargetHealth.TARGET_BOULDER;
    timer = 0;
}
```

In the previous code: we specify that the value of the variable called **type**, for the script called **ManageTargetHealth**, that is a component of the object **t** is **TARGET_BOULDER**.

Note that we have accessed the static variable **TARGET_BOULDER** from the class **ManageTargetHealth** without instantiating an object of type **ManageTargetHealth**; this is because the variable **TARGET_BOULDER** is static.

Last but not least, we can add the following code to the script **Bullet**.

```
if (coll.gameObject.tag == "target")
{
     //Destroy (coll.gameObject);
     coll.gameObject.GetComponent<ManageTargetHealth>().gotHit(10
);
     Destroy (gameObject);


}
```

You can now play the scene and test that the moving targets disappear after being hit twice.

For testing purposes, you can also drag and drop the script **ManageTargetHealth** on the prefab called **target**, reactivate the object **target** in the **Scene** view, and then fire bullets at this target. It should disappear after two bullets have been fired.

LEVEL ROUNDUP

In this chapter, we have learned how to create a simple level with a spaceship, for the player, that can fire missiles and destroy static or moving targets. We also managed to create moving targets spawn at regular intervals but at random locations. Finally, we also learned to create **Rigidbody2D** and **BoxCollider2D** components and detect collision between the player's bullets and the targets. So, we have covered considerable ground to get you started with the first level of your 2D shooter.

Checklist

You can consider moving to the next stage if you can do the following:

- Apply **Rigidbody2D** and **BoxCollider2D** components.

- Detect the keys pressed on the keyboard.

- Know the difference between **Input.GetKey** and **Input.GetKeyDown**.

- Apply a tag to an object.

- Understand how to generate random numbers.

- Detect collision from a script.

- Detect a tag from a script.

Quiz

Now, let's check your knowledge! Please answer the following questions (the answers are included in the resource pack) or specify if these statements are either correct or incorrect.

1. The method **Random.GenerateRandomNumber** is used to generate random numbers.

2. Sprites can be created using the menu **Create | Sprite**.

3. The function **Input.GetKeyDown** is called to detect when a key has been pressed and subsequently released.

4. The function **Input.GetKey** is called whenever a key is being pressed.

5. Static variables cannot be accessed outside their class.

6. The following code will add force to the **Rigidbody2D** component of the object linked to the script .

```
GetComponent<Rigidbody2D> ().AddForce (transform.up * 1000);
```

7. The following code will destroy 10 instances of the current object:

```
Destroy (gameObject, 10);
```

8. When a collision between two objects (each with a 2DCollider) occurs, the function **OnCollisionEnter2D** is called.

9. A function of type **void** does not return any value.

10. Only square sprites can be created in Unity.

Challenge 1

Now that you have managed to complete this chapter and that you have created your first level, you could improve the level by doing the following:

- Modify the color of each target.

- Modify the speed (or frequency) at which the moving targets are created.

Challenge 2

Now that you have managed to complete this chapter and that you have created your first level, you could improve it by doing the following:

- In the script **ManageTargetHealth**, create different types of targets; for example:

```
public static int TARGET_BOULDER_2 = 1;
```

- In the same script, modify the **Start** function so that the health of this particular target is set accordingly (i.e., different strength for different targets). For example:

```
If (type == ) health =;
```

- Modify the script **SpawnMovingTarget**, so that the boulder created is created at random; for example, you could generate a number between 1 and 2; based on this number, you will generate a boulder of type 0, or a boulder of type 1.

2
ADDING SPECIAL EFFECTS

In this section, we will learn how to create special effects for our initial game to provide more visual feedback to the player when targets have been hit, and to also provide the illusion of movement by adding a scrolling background.

After completing this chapter, you will be able to:

- Access and modify the color of objects at run-time to make them blink temporary.

- Create a simple scrolling background.

- Know how to use the **Sprite Editor**.

- Create animated images that will be used for explosions.

- Understand how to import and slice sprite sheets to create animations.

INTRODUCTION

In this chapter, we will learn how to create visual effects when the target has been hit (a blinking color) and destroyed (i.e., explosion). We will also create a scrolling background from a texture to give the impression of continuous movement.

ADDING SPECIAL EFFECTS TO THE TARGETS

In this section we will add some special effects when the targets are being hit.

When they are hit, they should blink blue. For this we will proceed as follows:

- When the object is hit, we will change its color to red.
- We will then start a timer that will count for 0.2 seconds.
- Once the .2 seconds have elapsed, we will then switch this object back to its original color.

So let's proceed:

- Please open the script called **ManageTargethealth**.

- Add this code at the beginning of the class.

```
public bool isBlinking = false;
public float timer;
public Color previousColor;
```

In the previous code:

- We declare three variables.

- The variable **isBlinking** will be used to determine if the object is blinking (i.e., if it is being hit).

- The variable **timer** will be used so that a new color is applied to this object for a few milliseconds; this will create a blinking effect.

- The variable **previousColor** will be used to save the color of the target before it starts to blink, so that this color can be applied again after the color change.

Please add this code in the **gotHit** function (new code in bold).

```
public void gotHit(int dammage)
{
    health-= dammage;
    if (health <= 0) destroyTarget ();
    previousColor = GetComponent<SpriteRenderer> ().color;
    GetComponent<SpriteRenderer> ().color = Color.blue;
    isBlinking = true;
```

In the previous code:

- The initial (i.e., the previous) color of the target is saved in the variable **previousColor**.

- The current color of the target is changed to **blue**.

- The variable **isBlinking** is set to **true**; it will be used to start a timer that will define when the blinking should stop (i.e., to determine how long the blue color should be applied for).

Finally, we just need to restore the previous color, after the delay has elapsed.

- Please add the following code to the **Update** function:

```
if (isBlinking)
{
    timer += Time.deltaTime;
    if (timer >= .2)
    {
        isBlinking = false;
        GetComponent<SpriteRenderer> ().color = previousColor;
        timer = 0;
    }
}
```

In the previous code:

- We check whether the sprite is in the blinking mode (i.e., if it is being hit).
- We then update the variable **timer** every frame.
- Once the time has reached .2 seconds, we then switch back to the original color for our sprite.

Please save the script, play the scene and check that upon firing at a target, its color turns to blue very briefly. For testing purposes, you can activate the object called target and fire at this target and see if it blinks upon being hit), as illustrated on the next figure.

Figure 31: The target blinks after being hit

ADDING AN EXPLOSION

Now that the blinking effect is working, we will create an explosion when the target is destroyed; for this purpose, we will use existing sprites, and then sequence them to create an animation (or an animated sprite); when the target is destroyed, this animated sprite will be spawn at the target's position and subsequently removed once the explosion animation is complete.

- Please open the resource pack provided with this book.

- Import the texture called **explosion.png** from the resource pack folder to the **Project** window in Unity (e.g., drag and drop).

- After importing the texture, Unity will create a new asset called **explosion** in the **Project** window.

Figure 32: Importing the explosion sprite sheet

- Using the **Inspector**, change its **Sprite Mode** properties to **Multiple**, as illustrated on the next figure:

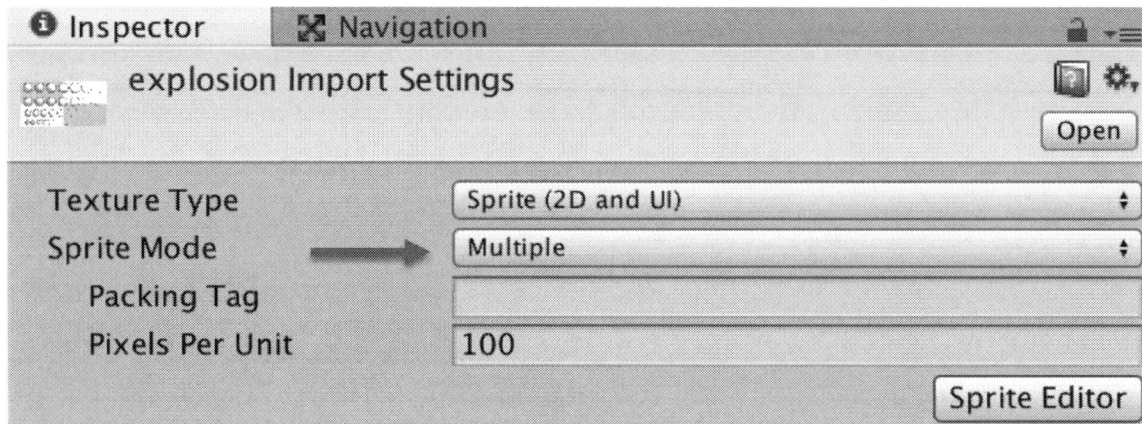

Figure 33: Importing the explosion sprite sheet

- By modifying this property, we indicate that this image includes possible sub-images to be generated for our animation.

- Please click on the button called **Apply** located in the bottom-right corner of the **Inspector** window, as described in the next figure.

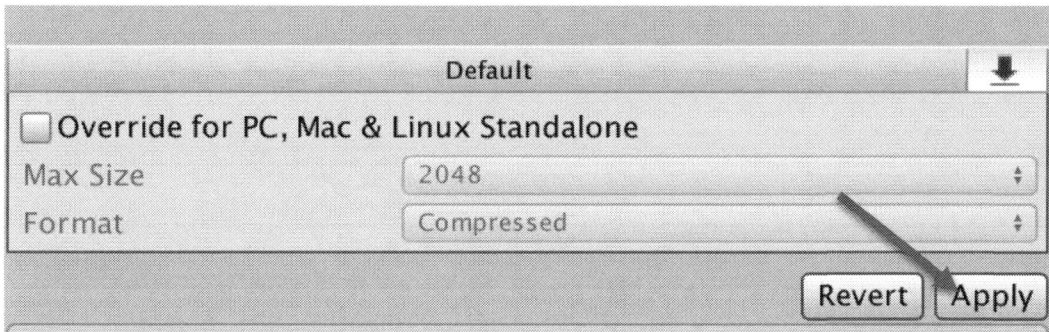

Figure 34: Applying changes

- Then click on the button called **Sprite Editor** (as illustrated on the next figure).

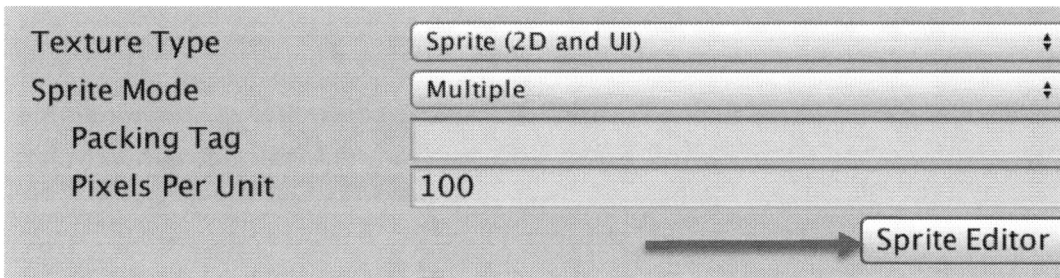

Figure 35: Opening the Sprite Editor (part 1)

- This should open the **Sprite Editor** window.

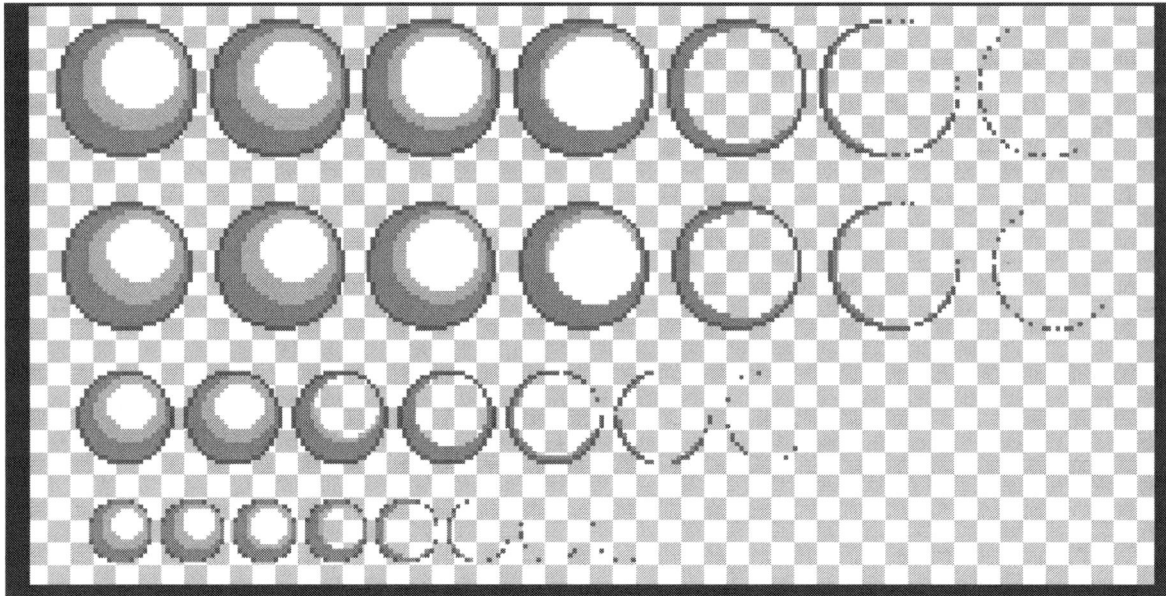

Figure 36: Opening the Sprite Editor (part 2)

The **Sprite Editor** makes it possible to edit sprites; in our case, we have imported a sprite sheet: an image made-up of other sub-images; what we want is to extract some of these images in order to create our animation. The idea is to "slice" this image (e.g., the sprite sheet) into sub-images and then to create an animation based on these "slices".

- When the **Sprite Editor** window opens, please click on the button called **Slice** located in the top-left corner of the **Sprite Editor** window.

Figure 37: Clicking the Slice button

- A new window will appear.

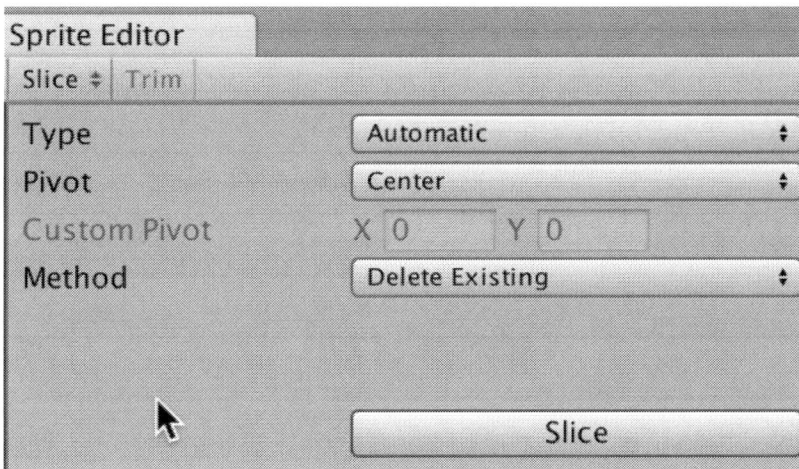

Figure 38: Slicing the sprite sheet (part 1)

- Please modify its settings as per the next figure.

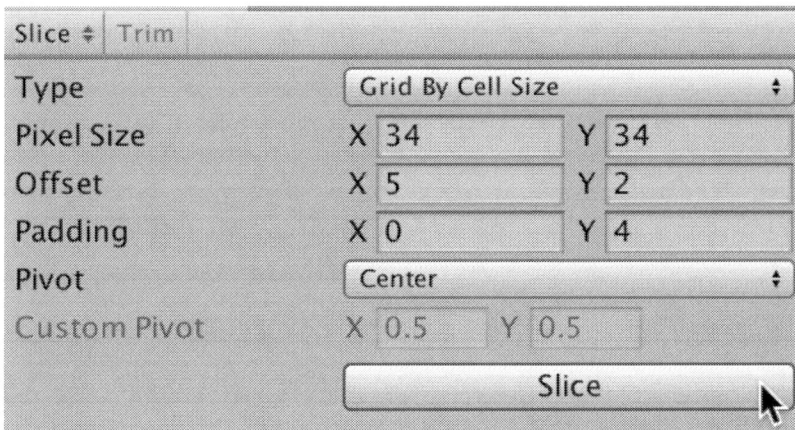

Figure 39: Slicing the sprite sheet (part 2)

The idea of this window is to specify how to capture the sub-images within.

- **Type**: By specifying "**Grid By Cell Size**" we mention that these are laid out as a grid.

- **Pixel Size**: Each sub-image (or sprite) is **34** by **34** pixels.

- **Offset**: For each row, there is a horizontal offset of 5 pixels and a vertical offset of 2 pixels from the start of the image (i.e., from the top-left corner).

- **Padding**: There is also padding between each cells, 0 horizontally and 4 pixels vertically.

- **Pivot**: If an image is rotated, the pivot used for this rotation will be its **center**, by default.

Once this is done, you can press the button called **Slice**, to actually slice the image.

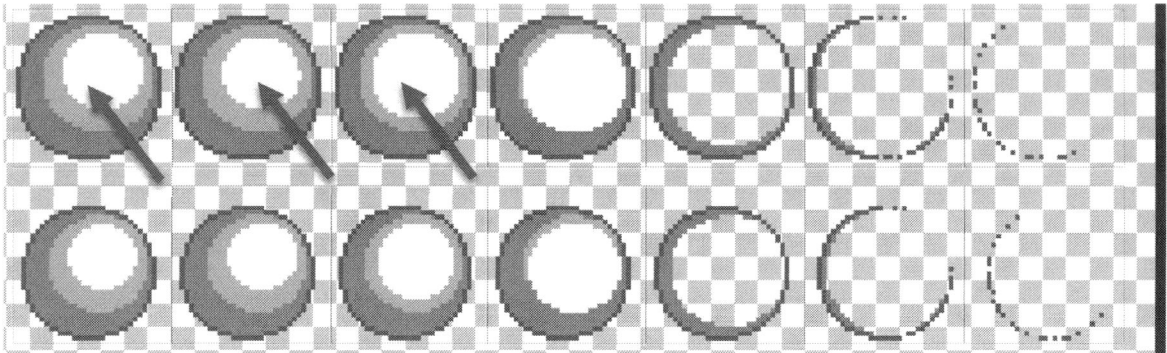

Figure 40: Slicing the sprite sheet (part 3)

- As you can see, we now have managed to define the sub-images from the original file. Each of these is defined by a grey square.

- Once this is done, you can, click on the button called **Apply** at the top of the **Sprite Editor** window.

Figure 41: Applying the slicing settings

- If you look in the **Project** window, you should now see that the original image for the explosion has now turned into a folder with several sprites.

Figure 42: The slices (sprites) from the original image

- If you click on the individual sprites in the list (e.g., **explosion_0**) and look at the **Inspector** window, you will be able to see what they look like; for example, **explosion_0**, may look like the next figure:

Figure 43: Visualizing the sprite explosion_0

Next, we will create an animation from the first seven sprites; if you remember well, the first row of the original image (i.e., the sprite sheet) included seven sprites that made up the animation that we needed; so now we will create an animation from these images.

Remember, an animation is a succession of sprites that, put together, give the illusion of movement.

- From the **Project** window, please select the seven first sprites (**explosion0**, **eplosion2**, ..., **explosion 6**) that we have created. To select all of these sprites, you can **left-click** on the first sprite (i.e., **explosion_0**), then press **CTRL** and then left-click on the six other sprites individually, as illustrated on the next figure. Alternatively, you can also **left-click** on the first sprite, and then press **SHIFT,** and left-click on the last sprite (i.e., **explosion_6**).

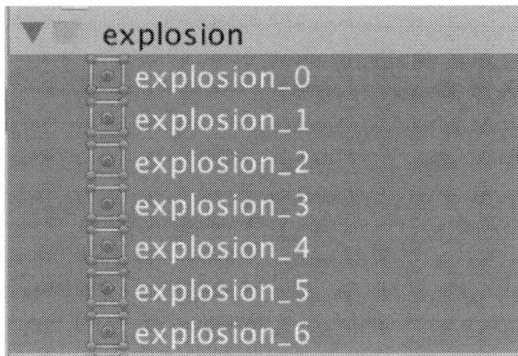

Figure 44: Selecting the seven sprites for the animation

- Once the seven sprites have been selected, please drag and drop these sprites to the **Scene** view, so that Unity can recognise this sequence of sprites (and save them) as an animation.

- As you drag these sprites to the **Scene** view, the mouse cursor will change to display the message <**Multiple**>, as illustrated on the next figure.

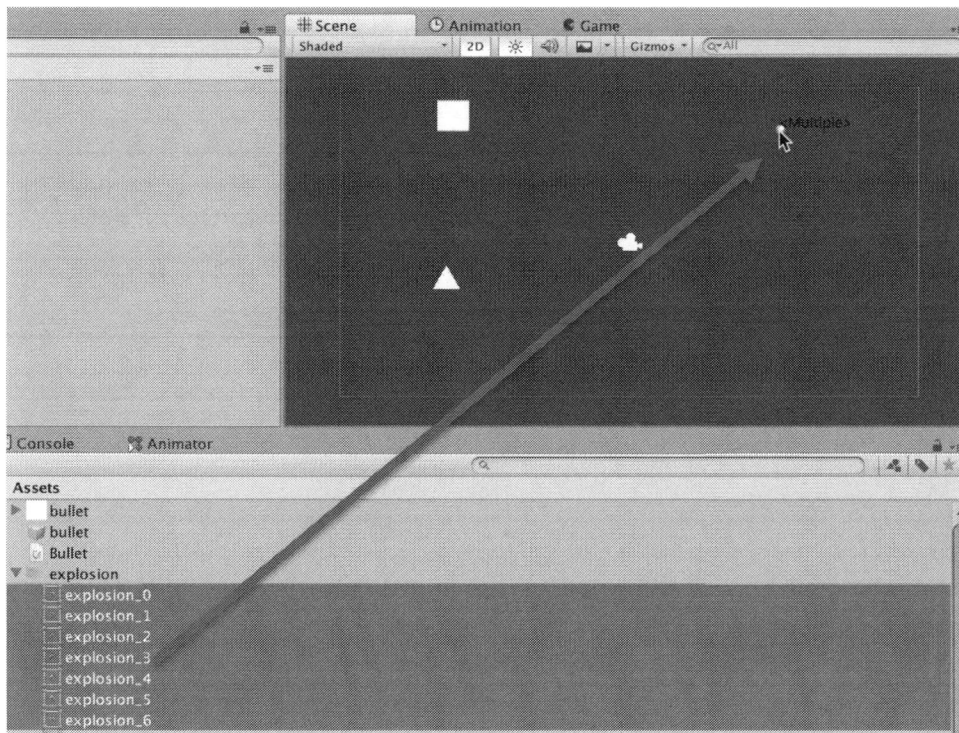

- Once you have dropped the sprites in the **Scene** view, a new window will appear, asking you to save the resulting animation.

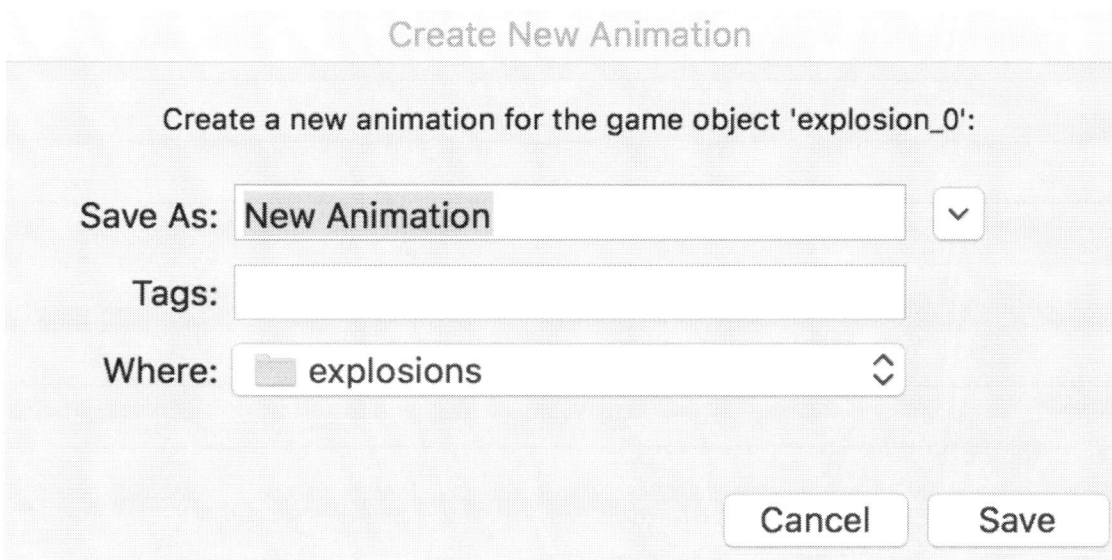

Figure 45: Saving the animation

- You can call this animation **explosion_animated_1** (or any other name of your choice) and then click on the button **Save**, in the same window.

- This will create three different assets: (1) a new object called **explosion_0** in the **Hierarchy**, (2) an animation called **explosion_animated_1** in the **Project** window, and (3) an **Animator Controller** called **explosion_0** in the **Project** window.

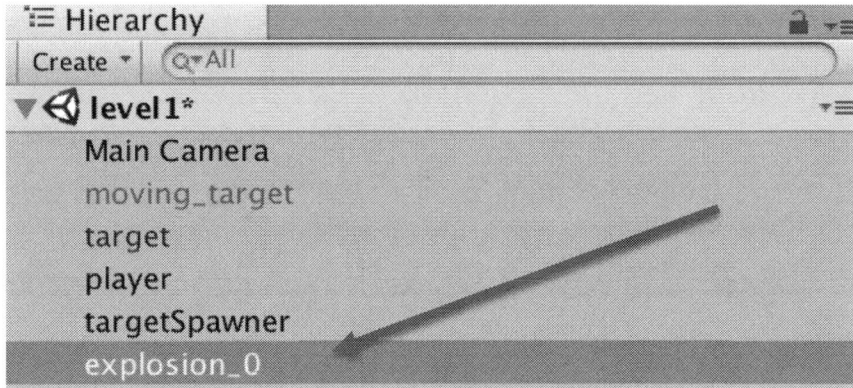

Figure 46: A new object created from the animation

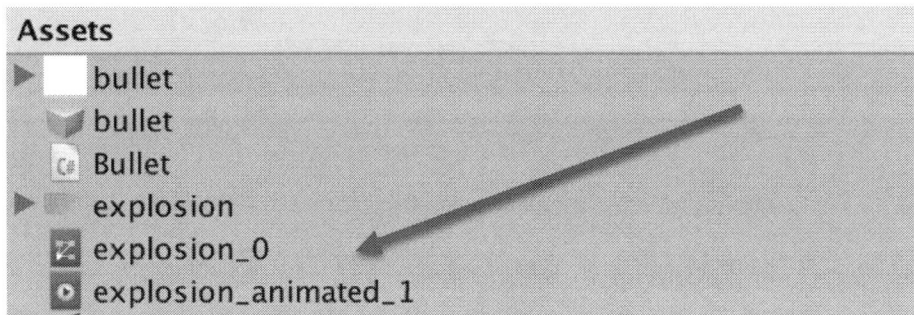

Figure 47: New assets created in the Project window

- In the **Hierarchy** window, please rename the object that you have just created (i.e., **explosion_0**) **explosion**.

If you play the scene, you should see the animated explosion, where you have dragged and dropped the animation in the scene.

You may also notice that the explosion is actually smaller than the target object; so we will rescale the explosion (so that it matches the size of the target) and also create a prefab from it.

- Please select the object called **explosion** in the **Hierarchy**, and, using the **Inspector**, change its scale to **(3.5, 3.5, 1)**;

You may also have noticed that this animation (i.e., the explosion) is looping continuously; however, for our game, we just want it to be played once; so we will modify the animation for the explosion.

- Using the **Project** window, locate the file called **explosion_animated_1**.

Note that you can use the search window located at the top of the **Project** to look for specific assets, and to find them quickly, as described in the next figure.

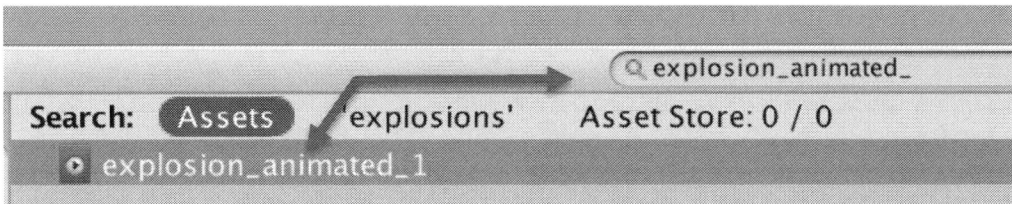

Figure 48: Looking for the explosion animation

- As you left-click on this asset in the **Project** window (i.e., **explosion_animated_1**), you can see its properties in the **Inspector** window.

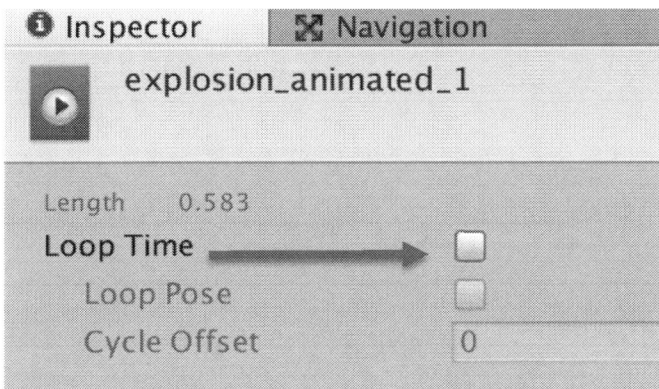

Figure 49: Modifying the explosion animation

- Please, set its attribute **Loop Time** to **false** (i.e., unticked); this means that the animation should not loop.

- Play the scene again, and you should see that the animation is played only once this time.

Once this is done, we just need to create a prefab from this explosion, as we will then instantiate this **explosion** prefab whenever a target is destroyed.

- Please clear the search field in the **Project** view, if you have used it earlier.

Figure 50: Clearing the search field for the Project view

- Please drag and drop the object called **explosion** from the **Hierarchy** to the **Project** window. This will create a new prefab called **explosion**.

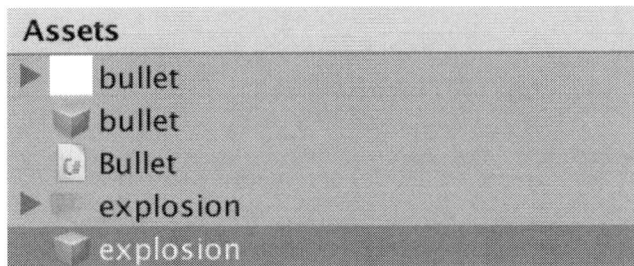

Figure 51: Creating the prefab called explosion

- You can then remove (i.e. delete or deactivate) the object called **explosion** form the **Hierarchy** now (since we have a corresponding prefab now). To do so, you can use the **SUP** or **DEL** keys on your keyboard.

We will then modify the script **ManageTargetHealth**, so that this prefab (i.e., **explosion**) is created at the point of impact between a bullet and a target.

- Please open the script **ManageTargetHealth**.

- Add the following code at the beginning of the script (new code in bold).

```
public float timer;
public Color previousColor;
public GameObject explosion;
```

- Add the following code to the function **destroyTarget** (new code in bold).

```
GameObject      exp      =      (GameObject)(Instantiate      (explosion,
transform.position, Quaternion.identity));
Destroy (exp, .5f);
Destroy (gameObject);
```

In the previous code:

- We instantiate an explosion.
- This explosion is then destroyed after .5 seconds.

Once this is done:

- Please save your script.

- In the **Project** window, select the prefab called **target**.

- Using the **Inspector**, scroll down to the component **ManageTargetHealth**.

- Click to the right of the attribute **Explosion**, as illustrated in the next figure

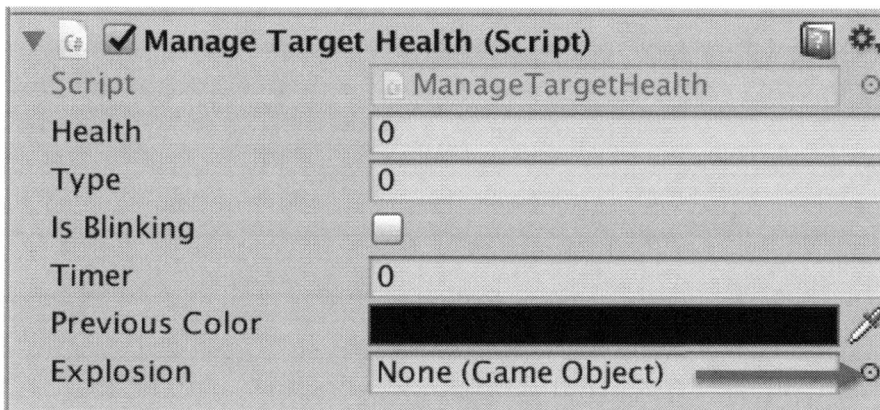

- Using the new window, search for and select the prefab called **explosion**.

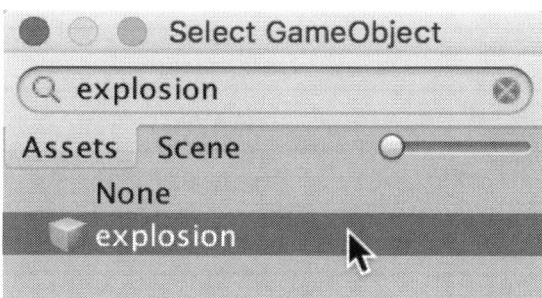

Figure 52: Selecting the explosion

Please repeat these steps for the prefab **moving_target**:

- In Unity, select the prefab **moving_target**.

- Using the **Inspector**, scroll down to the component **ManageTargetHealth**.

- Click to the right of the attribute **Explosion**.

- Using the new window, search and select the prefab called **explosion**.

Before we can play our scene, we can delete (or deactivate) the explosion that is already present in the scene.

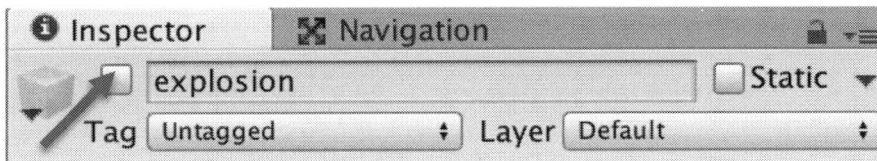

Figure 53: Deactivating the explosion present in the scene

Once this is done, you can play the scene. As you shoot at the static target, you should see an explosion after it has been hit twice; this explosion should then disappear after a few milliseconds.

CREATING A SCROLLING BACKGROUND

Ok, so now that we have created a moving object, we will start to create a moving background to give the illusion of movement; for this, we will do the following:

- Import a texture for our background.

- Modify its properties, so that it can be made scrollable.

- Apply this texture to a **Quad** object.

- Create a script that will make this texture scroll atop the **Quad** object.

So let's get started:

- Please locate the resource pack in your file system.

- Import the texture called **moving_bg_tile** to Unity's **Project** window.

Figure 54: Importing the scrolling background

Once this is done, please select this asset (i.e., **moving_bg_tile**) from the **Project** window and use the **Inspector** window to set its attributes as follows:

- **Texture Type: Texture** (we use a texture here, as textures can be made scrollable).

- **Wrap Mode: Repeat** (this is also so that the texture can be made scrollable).

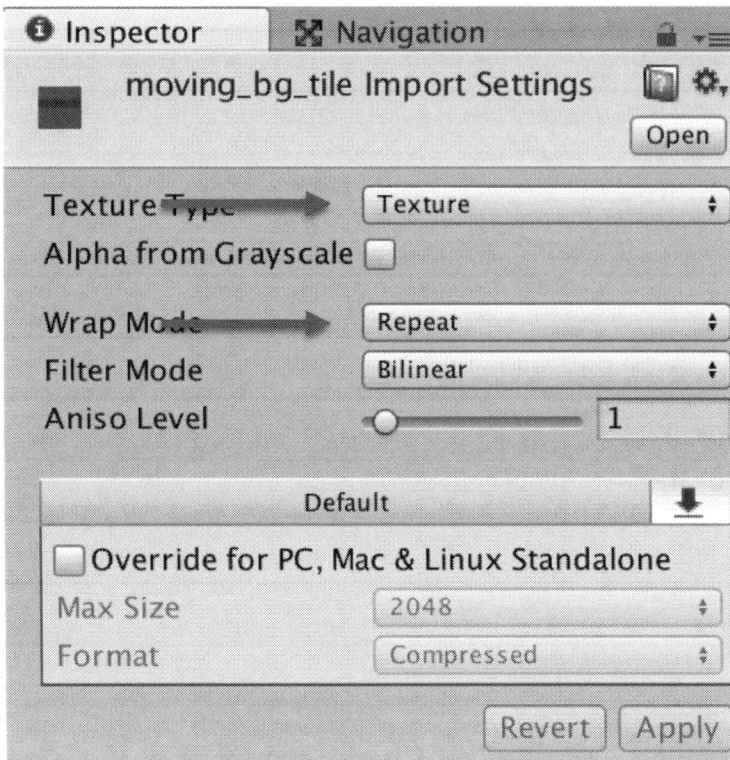

Figure 55: Setting the attributes of the scrolling background

- Once this is done, please click on the button **Apply** located at the bottom of the **Inspector** window, to apply these changes.

Next we will create a new object for our background and apply the texture to it:

- Please create a new **Quad** object (**GameObject | 3D Object | Quad**).

- Using the **Hierarchy**, rename this object **moving_background**.

- Drag and drop the texture **moving_bg_tile** from the **Project** window to this object in the **Hierarchy**.

- Rescale this object (i.e., **moving_background**) by changing its scale properties to **(40, 20, 1)**.

- Change its position to **(0, 0, 0)** so that its centre is close to the centre of the screen, as illustrated in the next figure.

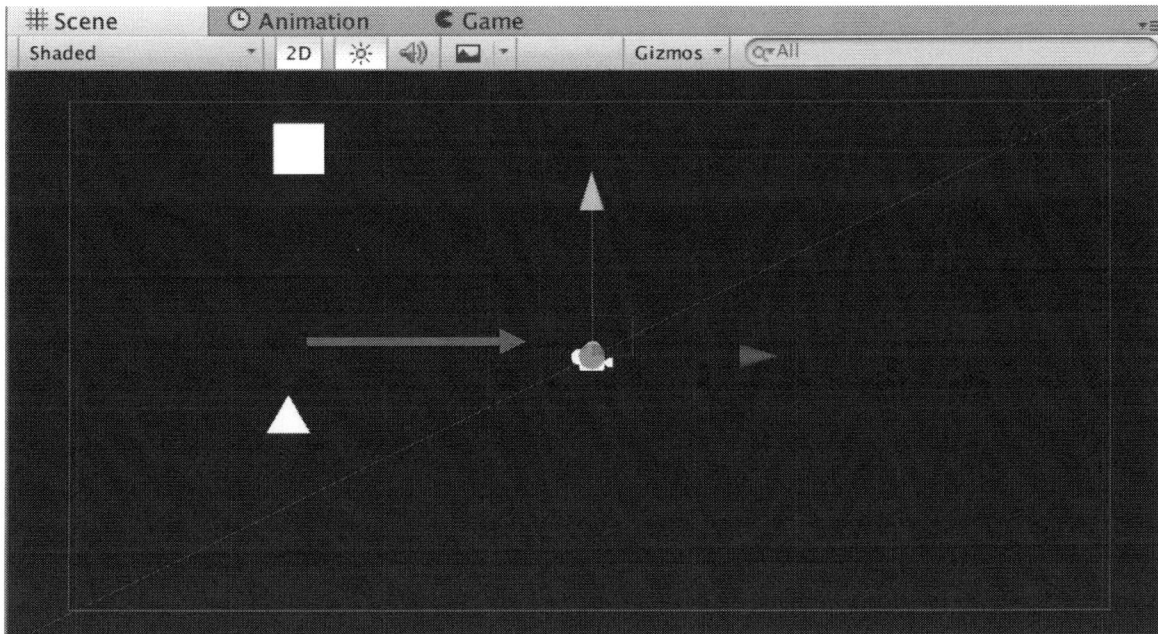

Figure 56: Aligning the moving background with the spaceship

- To check that this is correct, you can look at the game view, and check that the background fills-up the screen (if not, you can scale-up the background a bit more).

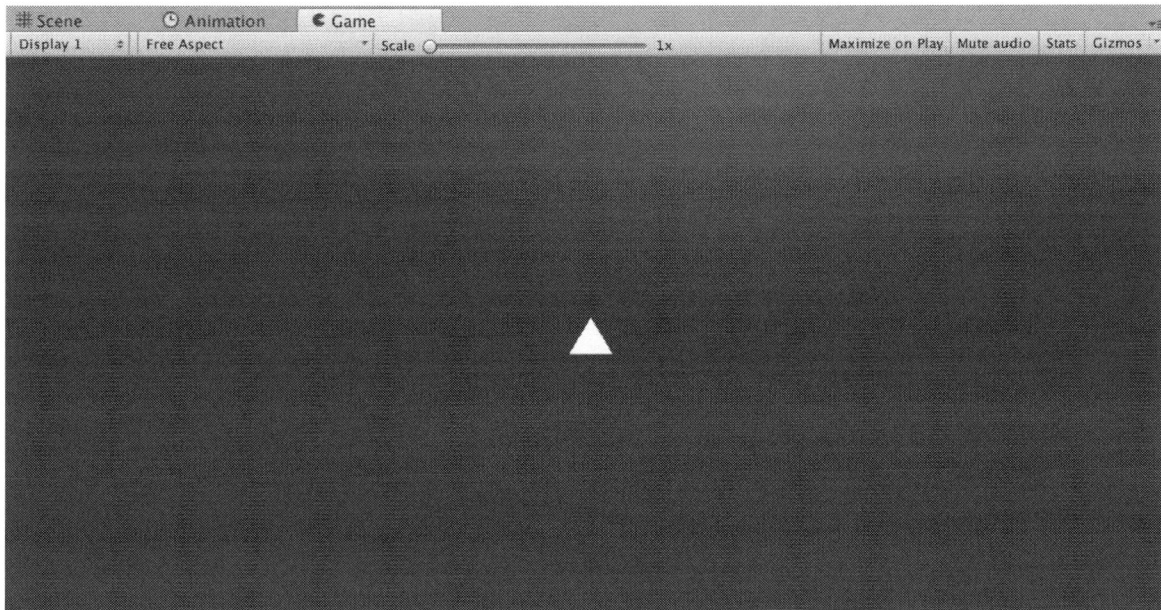

Figure 57: Checking the position of the moving background

Next, we will create a script that will perform the scrolling for us:

- Please create a new C# script and call it **ScrollingBackground**.

- Add the following code to it, in the function **Update** (new code in bold).

```
void Update ()
{
    GetComponent<Renderer>().material.mainTextureOffset  =  new
Vector2 (0,0.5f*Time.time);
}
```

In the previous code,

- We access the **Renderer** component of the object linked to the script. This component can be used to modify the way a texture is displayed; in our case, we will manage its vertical offset.

- We then access the main texture (the texture that we have just added to the Quad).

- We finally modify the vertical offset for this texture; in other words, we move it along the y-axis at .5 units per seconds (this would be 50 pixels per seconds, since our import settings for the background specified 100 pixels per units).

Once this is done; please save your code, check that it is error-free, and drag and drop this scrip on the object called **moving_background**.

- If you select the object **moving_background** in the **Hierarchy** and then look at the **Inspector** window, you should see that it includes the component **ScrollingBackground**.

Please play the scene and you should see that the background is actually scrolling vertically. However, you may also notice that the scene is quite dark, preventing you from seeing the background clearly.

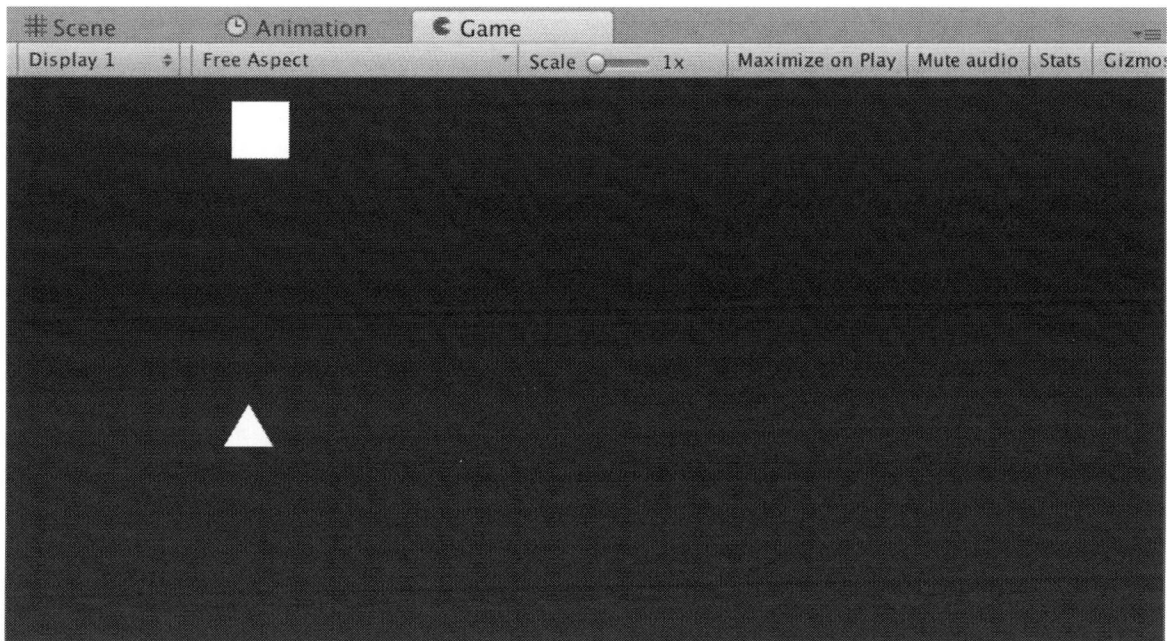

Figure 58: The scene before adding light

So we could add some light to the scene to solve this issue, as follows:

- Please select **GameObject | Light | Directional Light** from the top menu.

- This will create a new object called **Directional Light**.

- Rename this object **light**.

- Then, select it, and, using the **Inspector** window, change its rotation to **(0,0,0)** and its position to **(0,0,0)**. You can also change its intensity if you wish.

You can test the scene again and the scene should be much brighter.

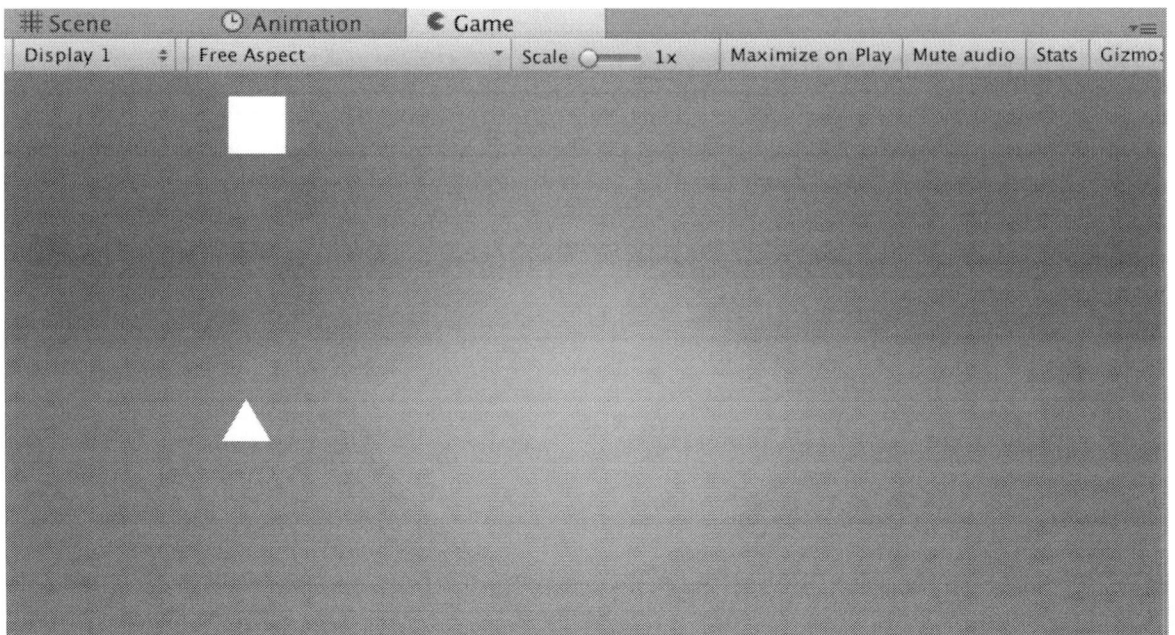

Figure 59: The scene after adding light

LEVEL ROUNDUP

Well, this is it!

In this chapter, we have learned about creating simple but powerful visual effects, including a blinking object, explosions made from sprites, along with a scrolling. So, we have, by now, a very simple but almost complete 2D shooter game.

Checklist

You can consider moving to the next chapter if you can do the following:

- Slice a sprite sheet.

- Create an animation from a sprite.

- Create a scrolling background.

Quiz

It's now time to check your knowledge with a quiz. So please try to answer the following questions (or specify whether the statements are correct or incorrect). The solutions are included in your resource pack. Good luck!

1. You can select multiple assets by using CTRL + left-click.

2. You can select multiple assets by using SHIFT + left-click.

3. You can modify (i.e., change the color of pixels of) a sprite using the **Sprite Editor**.

4. For an image to be sliced, its **Sprite Mode** attribute should be set to **Single**.

5. You can create a new button, by selecting **GameObject | Text** from the top menu.

6. The following code will change the color of a sprite to red.

```
GetComponent<SpriteRenderer> ().color = Color.red;
```

7. The following code will scroll a texture vertically.

```
GetComponent<Renderer>().material.mainTextureOffset = new Vector2
(0.5f*Time.time,0);
```

8. The following code will scroll a texture horizontally.

```
GetComponent<Renderer>().material.mainTextureOffset = new Vector2
(0,0.5f*Time.time);
```

9. To create an animation from existing sprites, you need to select these sprites, and then select: **GameObject | New Animation**.

10. To create a directional light, you can select: **GameObject | Light | Directional Light**.

Challenge 1

Now that you have managed to complete this chapter and that you have improved your skills, let's do the following:

- Create your own background with the image editor of your choice, and use it as a scrolling background for the game.

- Modify the blinking color and the blinking speed used when a target has been hit.

3
IMPROVING OUR GAME

In this section, we will improve our game by including additional features that will help to keep the spaceship onscreen, to manage its health levels, and to also make the game more challenging with some AI-driven NPCs.

After completing this chapter, you will be able to:

- Check if the player is in the field of view of the camera.

- Apply damage to the spaceship and manage the player's health.

- Include some artificial intelligence to the NPCs.

- Trigger attacks from the NPCs when the player is detected.

INTRODUCTION

In this chapter we will improve the current game by including a few add-ons:

- We will detect if the player is outside the camera's field of view and ensure that it is always visible.

- We will create NPCs, each with artificial intelligence, that will be moving horizontally and shoot at the player.

- We will also manage the player's health and detect when the spaceship has been hit or when it has collided with targets.

KEEPING THE PLAYER IN THE FIELD OF VIEW

So, all works well so far; the only thing is that, as you may have noticed, the player might be going off-screen, at times, and become invisible; so we will build a mechanism that will solve this issue; we will proceed as follows:

- We will need to detect when the player is no longer in the camera's field of view.

- For this purpose, we will need to translate the **world position** of the player into its position in relation to the camera view.

- So, we will convert the position of the player to the actual camera view port.

- We will then ensure that this position, in the camera view, is within the field of view of the camera; the position of the player, if the player is outside the view, may be modified if need be, so that it is no less that 0, but no more than 1. This is because, the position of objects, in the camera view, is using x and y coordinates that range from 0 to 1; for example, along the x-axis, 0 means the left side of the screen, and 1, means the right side of the screen.

- Once we have made sure that the player is in the field of view, we can then convert this position from the referential defined by the camera view (between 0 and 1) to a world position (from 0 to infinity).

Ok, so let's get started:

- Please open the script called **MovePlayer**.

- Add the following code to the function **Update** (at the end of the function).

```
Vector3                      viewPortPosition                      =
Camera.main.WorldToViewportPoint(transform.position);
viewPortPosition.x = Mathf.Clamp01(viewPortPosition.x);
viewPortPosition.y = Mathf.Clamp01(viewPortPosition.y);
transform.position                                                 =
Camera.main.ViewportToWorldPoint(viewPortPosition);
```

In the previous code:

- We define a new vector called **viewPortPosition**; this vector will be used to define the position of the object in relation to the camera view.

Note that, in the camera view (or **viewport**), objects' positions are expressed using x and y coordinates that range between 0 and 1; for the x coordinate 0 means the left side of the screen and 1 means the right side of the screen. For the y coordinate 1 means the top of the screen and 0 means the bottom of the screen.

- We then clamp the value of both x and y coordinates; in other words, we ensure that their values are within 0 and 1 (i.e., onscreen); this is done using the built-in function **Clamp01**.

- We then translate this position from the camera view (or viewport) to world coordinates using the function **ViewportToWorldView**.

In the previous code, what we have effectively done is a change of referential from the world view, to the camera view, and then back to the world view.

Please check your code and test the scene, you will notice that the player is now always onscreen; however, only half of the player is displayed when you try to move beyond the camera view, as illustrated in the next figure.

Figure 60: Improving position clamping

We could fix this as follows:

- Determine the size of our sprite on the x- and y–axis.

- Calculate how this size can be translated in the view port settings (i.e., what proportion of the screen the sprite would occupy).

- Clamp the player to the size of the screen (height or width) minus the size of the sprite.

- Translate this clamping to world view coordinates.

Please add (or comment) the following code to the script **MovePlayer** (new code in bold):

```
//Vector3                    viewPortPosition                    =
Camera.main.WorldToViewportPoint(transform.position);
//viewPortPosition.x = Mathf.Clamp01(viewPortPosition.x);
//viewPortPosition.y = Mathf.Clamp01(viewPortPosition.y);
//transform.position                                             =
Camera.main.ViewportToWorldPoint(viewPortPosition);


Vector3                     viewPortPosition                     =
Camera.main.WorldToViewportPoint(transform.position);
Vector3                     viewPortXDelta                       =
Camera.main.WorldToViewportPoint(transform.position            +
Vector3.left/2);
Vector3                     viewPortYDelta                       =
Camera.main.WorldToViewportPoint(transform.position            +
Vector3.up/2);
```

In the previous code:

- We comment the previous code.

- We create two new vectors: **viewPortXDelta** and **viewPortYDelta**.

- **viewPortXDelta** will be used to determine the relative size of the sprite along the x axis (i.e., its width). Note that we use **Vector3.left/2** because we want to know the distance between the center of the sprite and its edges (i.e., half its width).

- **viewPortYDelta** will be used to determine the relative size of the sprite along the y axis (i.e., its height). Note that we use **Vector3.up/2** because we want to know the distance between the center of the sprite to its edge (half its height).

Note that our sprite, at present, has a scale of 1 on all axes; so the magnitude (length) of the vectors **Vector3.up** or **Vector3.left** will effectively describe the width or height of this sprite; however, if the scale had been **2** on the x axis, for example, we would then need to use **Vector3.left** instead of **Vector3.left/2 (i.e., Vector3.left/2** multiplied by 2).

- Please add the following code in the same **Update** function (new code in bold), just after the previous code:

```
float deltaX = viewPortPosition.x - viewPortXDelta.x;
float deltaY = -viewPortPosition.y + viewPortYDelta.y;

viewPortPosition.x = Mathf.Clamp(viewPortPosition.x, 0+deltaX, 1-deltaX);
viewPortPosition.y = Mathf.Clamp(viewPortPosition.y, 0+deltaY, 1-deltaY);
transform.position                                                      =
Camera.main.ViewportToWorldPoint(viewPortPosition);
```

In the previous code:

- We declare two variables called **deltaX** and **deltaY**; these will be used to determine the actual distance, in the viewport, between the center of the sprite and its edges.

- We then clamp the position of the sprite using the values that we have calculated earlier; so the minimum x position will be the left side of the screen + half the width of the sprite; the same is done with the y position; all of these changes are done in the viewport referential (i.e., values ranging between 0 and 1)

- As we have done before, these new coordinates are then translated to world view coordinates.

Please save your code and check that it is error-free, and test your game; as you move towards the edges of the screen, you should now see that the player is properly "clamped" to each side of the screen, and that the full triangle is now displayed.

Figure 61: Clamping the player to the bottom-left corner

That's it!

APPLYING DAMAGE TO THE PLAYER

In this section, we will create code to implement a feature whereby, when the moving targets collide with the player, they destroy the player; in this case, the level should also be restarted automatically.

The process will be as follows:

- We will add collision capabilities to our player.

- We will then detect collision with moving targets.

- We will finally restart the level in case of a collision.

So let's get to it:

- Please add a **Polygon2DCollider** to the player: select the **player** in the **Hierarchy**, then select **Component | Physic2D| Polygon2DCollider** from the top menu. This will add a **Polygon2DCollider** to the object, as illustrated on the next figure.

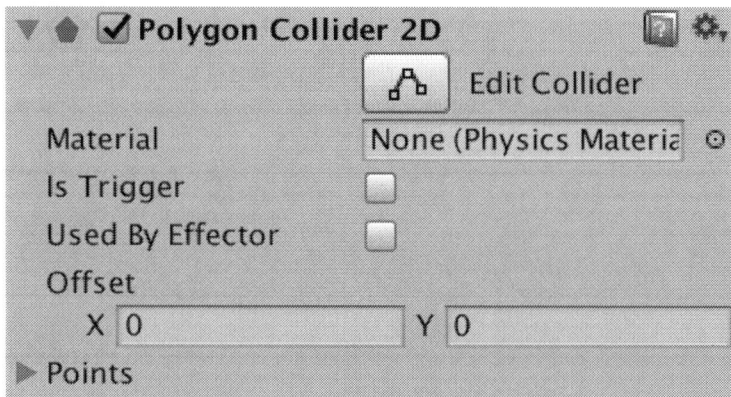

Figure 62: Adding a polygonal collider to the player

In the next sections, the player may be hit by other objects; so the mechanism involved in destroying the player and restarting the game may need to be performed several times (depending on the object that collided with the player); so to centralize this process and to make our code more efficient, we will create a function that manages this aspect of the game (i.e., player colliding with other objects), and add it to a script linked to the player. This way, upon collision with any object, this function will be called accordingly.

- Please create a new script called **ManagePlayerHealth**.

- Add the following code at the beginning of the class.

```
using UnityEngine.SceneManagement;
```

- Add the following functions at the end of the script (i.e., before the last closing curly bracket).

```
void OnCollisionEnter2D(Collision2D coll)
{
    if (coll.gameObject.tag == "target")
    {
        Destroy (coll.gameObject);
        DestroyPlayer ();
    }


}
void DestroyPlayer()
{
    SceneManager.LoadScene (SceneManager.GetActiveScene().name);
}
```

In the previous code:

- We detect collisions with targets.

- In case the player collides with a target, the target is destroyed, and the function called **DestroyPlayer** is called.

- The function **DestroyPlayer** reloads the current scene.

We can now apply this script:

- Please save your script and check that it is error-free.

- Drag and drop this new script (**ManagePlayerHealth**) on the object called **player** in the **Hierarchy**.

- Once this is done, you can test your scene and check that upon colliding with a moving target, that the scene is restarted.

Adding Artificial Intelligence

So at this stage, the game works relatively well, and we could also add a bit more challenge to it. So, to make this game more challenging to the player, we will add a few NPCs that will move and attack the player.

The NPC that we will add will be moving horizontally from left to right and it will shoot at the player whenever it is in front of the player (or close to it). It will consist of a simple triangle (the same as we have used for the player), that shoots projectiles towards the player, if the latter is detected.

- From the **Project** window, please drag and drop the asset called **Triangle** to the **Scene** view, as illustrated on the next figure.

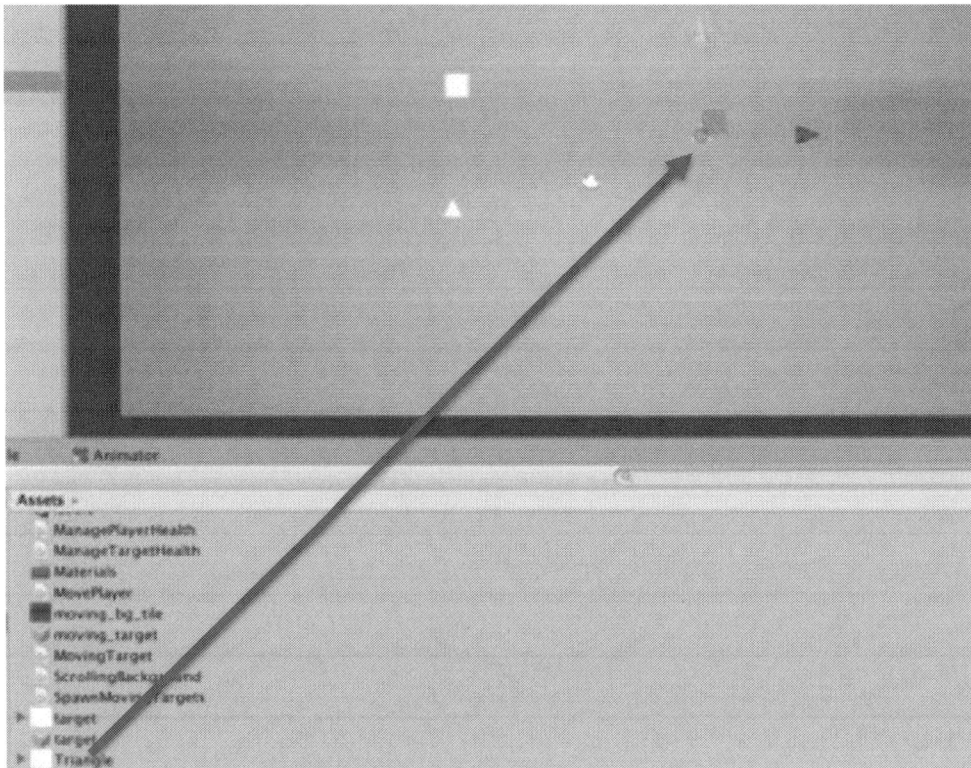

Figure 63: Recycling the triangle to create an NPC.

- This will create a new object called **Triangle** in the **Hierarchy** window.

- Please rename this object **npc1**.

- Using the **Inspector**, change the rotation of this object to **(0, 0, 180),** so that it looks like the next figure.

Figure 64: Rotating the NPC

- Add a **Polygon Collider2D** to this object: select the object **npc1**, and then select the option **Components | Physics2D | PolygonCollider2D** from the top menu.

- Change its tag to **target**, as we have done previously using the **Inspector** window.

At this stage, we just need to make sure that this object, (i.e., **npc1**), can be destroyed in the same way as the targets that we have created earlier. So we will reuse the script called **ManageTargetHealth**, that was previously employed for the other targets.

- Please add the script **ManageTargetHealth** to the object **npc1** (i.e., drag and drop the script from the **Project** window to the object **npc1** in the **Hierarchy**).

- Select the object **npc1**, and then, using the **Hierarchy** window, click to the right of the attribute **Explosion** for the component **ManageTargetHealth**, as illustrated on the next figure.

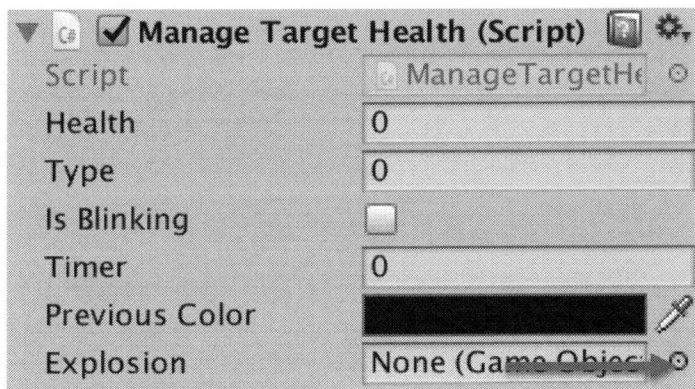

Figure 65: Adding an explosion

- Using the new window, search and select the prefab called **explosion**.

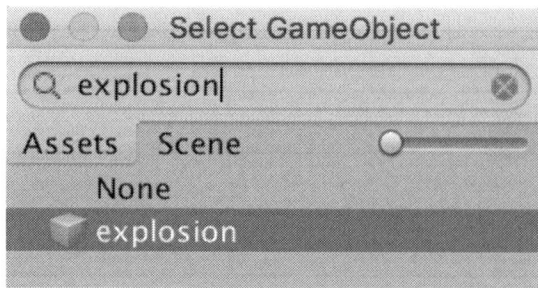

Figure 66: Choosing an explosion for the NPC

Next, we will create a new script that will be attached to the NPC; in this script, we will add some code that moves the NPC from right to left, and that also ensures that the NPC shoots at the player when it is in front of the player.

- Please create a new script called **MoveNPC**.

- Add the following code at the beginning of the class (new code in bold):

```
public class MoveNPC : MonoBehaviour {
public GameObject bullet;
public float direction = 1.0f;
public float timer;
```

In the previous code:

- We declare three variables.

- The variable **bullet** will be used as a placeholder for the bullet that we want to instantiate when the NPC shoots.

- The variable **direction** will be used to determine in what direction the NPC will be moving.

- The variable **timer** will be employed to determine when the NPC changes direction (e.g., from right to left or vice-versa).

- Please add the following code to the **Update** function.

```
timer += Time.deltaTime;
transform.Translate (Vector3.left *direction* Time.deltaTime *
2);
if (timer >= 2) {direction *= -1; timer = 0;}
```

In the previous code:

- We increase the variable **timer** by one, every seconds.

- Every second, we also move the NPC horizontally; it is moved to the left initially, as the value of the variable **direction** is **1** at the beginning.

- Then, after 2 seconds, the **direction** is reversed, and the **timer** is initialized back to **0**; so changes in the direction will occur every two seconds.

We can now save our script:

- Please save your code, and check that it is error-free.

- You can then drag and drop this script (i.e., **MoveNPC**) on the object **npc1**.

Once this done you can test the scene:

- Please deactivate the object **target** (i.e., f this is not already done).

- Move the object **npc1** to the upper boundary of the screen, as illustrated on the next figure.

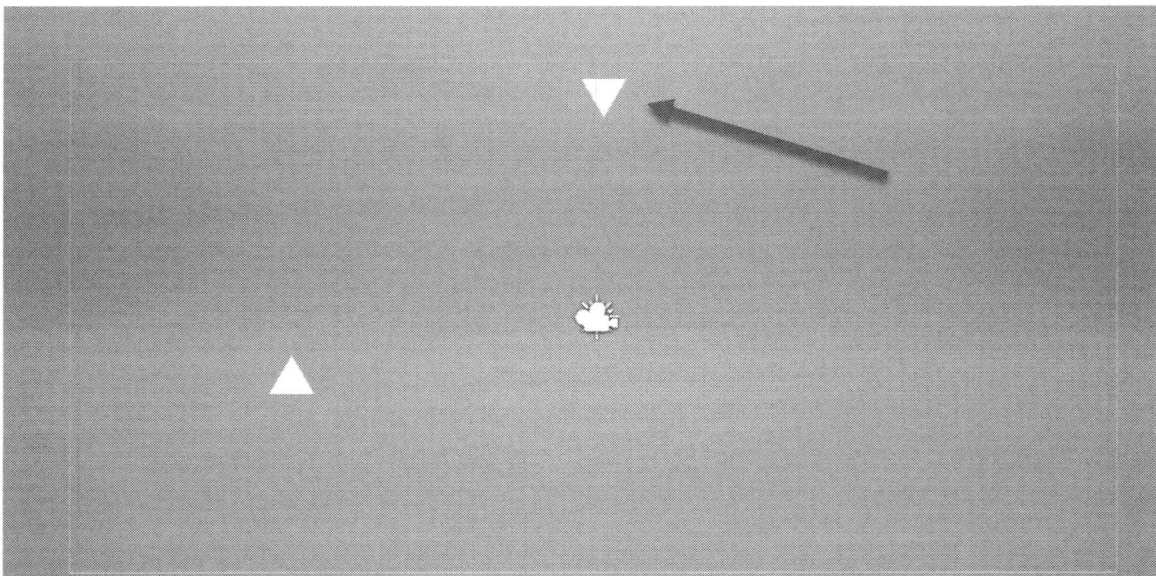

Figure 67: Moving the NPC

- As you play the scene, you should see that the NPC moves from left to right, as illustrated on the next figure.

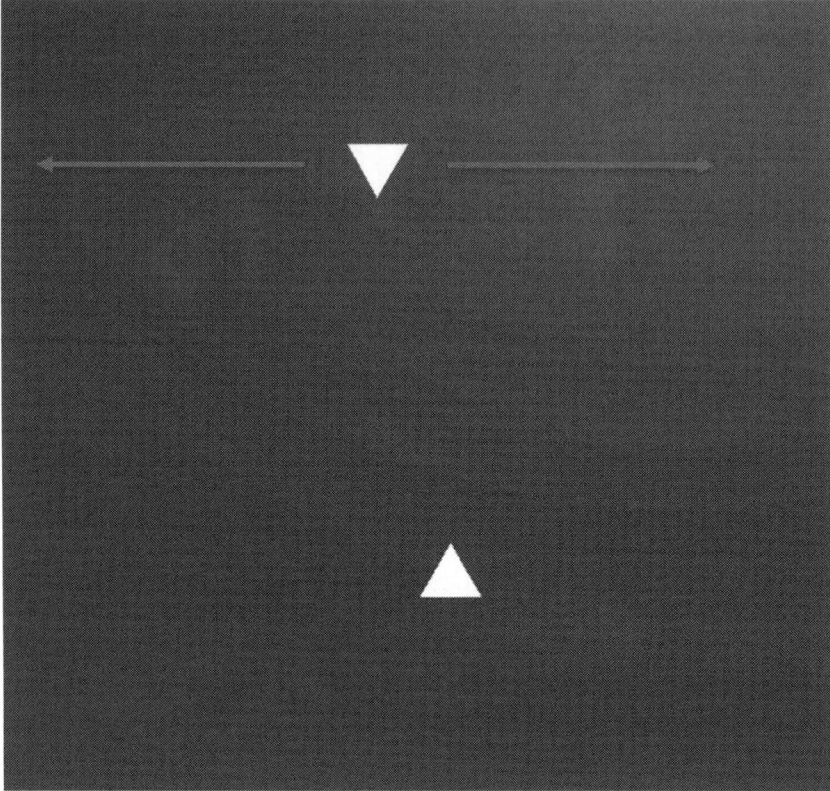

Figure 68: Testing the NPC's movement

Ok, so now that the NPC can move properly, we will add a feature whereby it shoots at the player when in front of the player. For this purpose, we will proceed as follows:

- Detect when the **NPC** is in front of the player.

- Shoot (i.e., instantiate a bullet prefab that moves towards the player).

- Ensure that the shooting stops after a few milliseconds, when the player is no longer in front of the NPC.

So let's start with this feature:

- Please open the script **MoveNPC**.

- Please add the following code to the function **Update** (new code in bold).

```
void Update ()
{
    timer += Time.deltaTime;
    transform.Translate (Vector3.left *direction* Time.deltaTime
* 2);
    if (timer >= 2) {direction *= -1; timer = 0;}
    detectPlayer ();
```

This function (i.e., **detectPlayer**) will be called to check if the player is in front of the NPC.

Now let's declare this function by adding the following code to the class, just after the function **Update**.

```
void detectPlayer()
{
    float           playerXPosition       =           GameObject.Find
("player").transform.position.x;
    if (transform.position.x < (playerXPosition + 1) &&
transform.position.x > (playerXPosition - 1)) Shoot();
}
```

In the previous code, we calculate the player's position on the **x-axis** and we then call the function called **shoot** if the player is in front of the NPC.

We just need to implement the function called **Shoot** now.

- Please add the following code at the end of the class, just after the previous function:

```
void Shoot()
{
    GameObject    b    =    (GameObject)(Instantiate    (bullet,
transform.position + transform.up*1.5f, Quaternion.identity));
    b.GetComponent<Rigidbody2D> ().AddForce (Vector3.down   *
1000);
}
```

In the previous code

- We define a new function called **Shoot**.

- We create a new object called **b** that is based on the variable **bullet** (the variable **bullet** will be initialized later using the **Inspector**).

- This projectile (i.e., the object called **b**) is then propelled downwards, by accessing its **Rigidbody2D** component and by then exerting a downwards force.

Please save your script and check that it is error-free.

Once this is done, we can now initialize the variable **bullet** defined in this script from the **Inspector**:

- Please, select the object **npc1** in the **Hierarchy**.

- Using the **Inspector**, click to the right of the attribute called **Bullet** for the script **MoveNPC**, as described on the next figure.

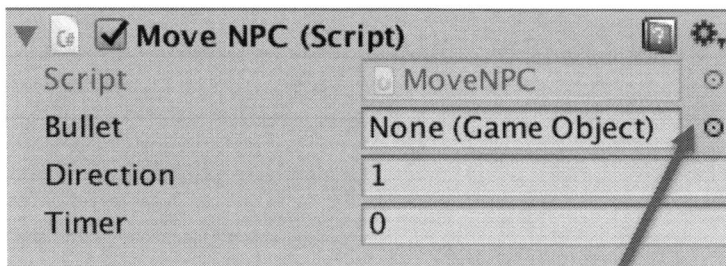

Figure 69: Selecting a bullet for the NPC (part 1)

- Using the new window, search and select the prefab called **bullet**.

Figure 70: Selecting a bullet for the NPC (part 2)

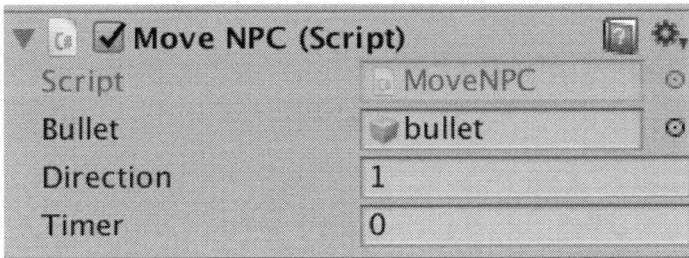

Figure 71: Selecting a bullet for the NPC (part 3)

Now that it is done, you can test the scene and check that the NPC fires bullets in the direction of the player when the player is in front of the NPC.

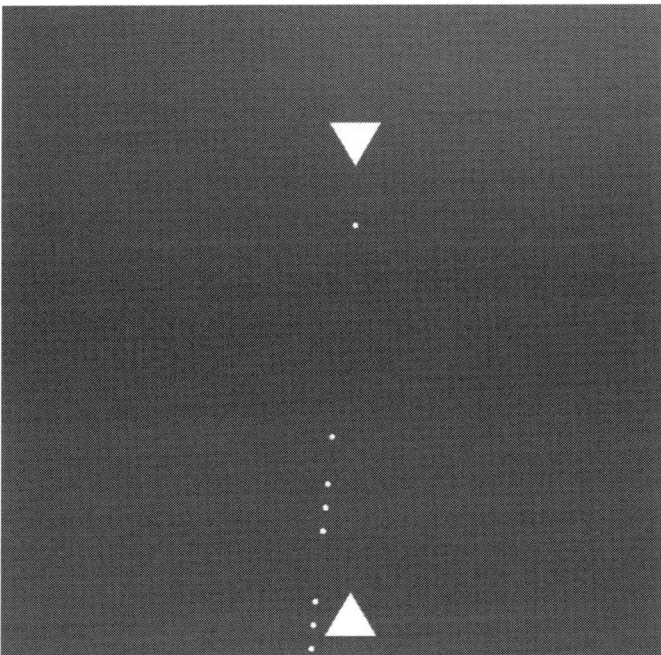

Figure 72: The NPC firing at the player

Now, this works well; however, there are a few things that we could improve, including:

- A slower firing rate for the NPC.

- Collision detection with the NPC's bullets.

- Restarting the level when the player has been shot.

Now, to start with, we will make sure that the game restarts if the player is hit by a bullet; to do so, we just need to add a tag to the bullets fired by the NPC, and then modify the script called **ManagePlayerHealth** to detect collision with these bullets. So, let's proceed:

- Please select the prefab called **Bullet** in the **Project** window.

- Create a new tag called **bullet**, as we have done earlier.

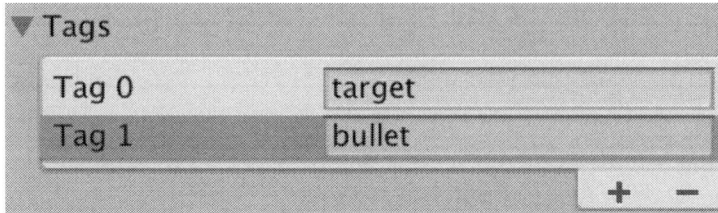

Figure 73: Creating a new tag for bullets

- Apply this tag to the prefab called **bullet**.

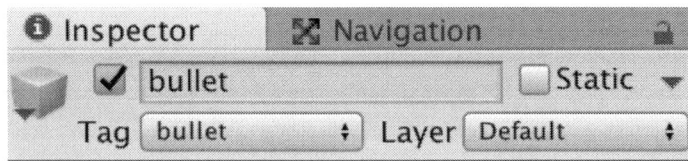

Figure 74: Applying the new tag to the bullet prefab

- Once this is done, please open the script **ManagePlayerHealth**.

- Modify the function **OnCollisionEnter2D** as follows (new code in bold):

```
void OnCollisionEnter2D(Collision2D coll)
{
    if (coll.gameObject.tag == "target" || coll.gameObject.tag
== "bullet")
    //if (coll.gameObject.tag == "target")
    {
        Destroy (coll.gameObject);
        DestroyPlayer ();
    }
}
```

In the previous code, we check that the object colliding with the player is either a moving target or a bullet.

Please save your code, check that it is error-free, and then test the scene.

Now that this is working, we can look at the NPC's firing rate: as you test the scene, you may notice that the firing rate of the NPC is quite high; so you can either leave it as it is or modify it, by amending the script **MoveNPC** as follows:

- Please open the script **MoveNPC**.

- Add the following code at the beginning of the class.

```
public bool startShootingTimer = false;
public bool canShoot = true;
public float shootingTimer;
```

- In the previous code, we create three variables that will be used to determine when the NPC can shoot again.

- Please add this code at the beginning of the **Update** function:

```
if (startShootingTimer)
{
    shootingTimer += Time.deltaTime;
    if (shootingTimer >= .5)
    {
        startShootingTimer = false;
        canShoot = true;
        shootingTimer = 0;
    }
}
```

In the previous code:

- If the NPC has just fired a bullet (i.e., **startShootingTimer** is true), the timer is ticking and its value is increased every second by one.

- If the timer reaches 500 milliseconds, then the timer stops ticking (i.e., **startShootingTimer** is false), and the player can shoot again.

- The timer is also reset to 0.

Now, we just need to modify the function **Shoot**, so that the **timer** starts just after the NPC has fired a bullet and also so that the NPC cannot shoot another bullet for the next 500 milliseconds (i.e., as long as the timer has not reached 500 milliseconds).

- Please modify the function called **Shoot**, in the script **MoveNPC**, as follows (new code in bold):

```
void Shoot()
{
     if (canShoot)
     {
          GameObject    b    =    (GameObject)(Instantiate    (bullet,
transform.position + transform.up * 1.5f, Quaternion.identity));
          b.GetComponent<Rigidbody2D> ().AddForce (Vector3.down
* 1000);
          canShoot = false;
          startShootingTimer = true;
     }

}
```

As you save and complete the code, you may test the scene and check that the NPC fires at a lower rate.

There is one more thing that we could modify in our game: as it is, several of the moving targets may fall on the NPC; however, we could decide to ignore collisions between these boulders and the NPC, otherwise, these targets may accumulate at the top of the screen. To do so, we will employ a built-in function called **IgnoreCollision** that will be used on every new moving target, so that collisions between NPCs and moving targets are ignored.

So let's proceed:

- Please create a new C# script called **IgnoreCollision**.

- Open this script.

- Add the following code to the function **Start** (new code in bold):

```
void Start ()
{
     Physics2D.IgnoreCollision    (GetComponent<BoxCollider2D>(),
GameObject.Find ("npc1").GetComponent<PolygonCollider2D> ());
}
```

In the previous code, we use the function **Physics2D.IgnoreCollision** to ignore collisions between the collider from the moving target (this object will be attached to this script) and the collider from the object with the name **npc1**. Although this function has some limitations when used with more than two objects (and we will see how this can be solved later), it is fine for the time being.

Please save your code, and check that the moving targets are not colliding anymore with the NPCs.

Once this is working, the next step will be to instantiate several NPCs at random positions; for example, we could instantiate one of these NPCs at the top of the screen, every 5 seconds; for this purpose, we will proceed as follows:

- We will create an empty object called **NPCSpawner**, that will be in charge of spawning NPCs.

- We will then set-up the **NPCSpawner** object so that NPCs are spawned at regular intervals.

So let's get started:

- Please create a prefab from the object called **npc1** (i.e., drag and drop the object **npc1** to the **Project** window); this will create a prefab called **npc1**.

Figure 75: The new prefab called npc1

- You can delete (or deactivate) the object called **npc1** from the **Hierarchy** window now.

- Please create a new empty object and rename it **NPCSpawner**.

- Create a new C# script called **SpawnNPCs** and drag and drop it to the object **NPCSpawner** in the **Hierarchy**.

We can now modify this script:

- Please open the script **NPCSpawner**.

- Add this code at the beginning of the class (new code in bold).

```
public class NPCSpawner : MonoBehaviour {
    public GameObject npc1;
    private float timer, respawnTime;
```

- In the previous code, we declare two variables that will be used to spawn NPCs at regular intervals.

- Please add this code to the **Update** function.

```
void Update ()
{
    timer += Time.deltaTime;
    if (timer >= 1)
    {
        timer = 0;
        SpawnNPC (npc1);


    }
}
```

- In the previous code, we create a timer that is used to spawn a new NPC every second.

- Please add this code at the end of the class (i.e., just before the last closing curly bracket):

```
void SpawnNPC(GameObject typeOfNPC)
{
    float range = Random.Range (-10, 10);//Screen.width);
    Vector3        newPosition        =        new        Vector3
(GameObject.Find("player").transform.position.x    +    range,
transform.position.y, 0);
    GameObject    newNPC    =    (GameObject)(Instantiate    (npc1,
newPosition,  Quaternion.identity));
    newNPC.transform.Rotate (new Vector3 (0, 0, 180));
    newNPC.name = "npc1";

}
```

In the previous code:

- We declare a variable called **range**, with a random value that will range between -10 and +10.

- This random value is then used to instantiated a new NPC for which the **x coordinate** is based on the x coordinate of the player +/- 10; this is similar to the code used to instantiate moving targets.

- The name of the new NPCs that has been instantiated is set to **npc1**.

You can now save your script and set-up the **NPCSpawner** object:

- Please, save your script.

- Using the **Hierarchy**, please select the object **NPCSpawner**.

- In the **Inspector**, you will see a field called **NPC1** for the component called **NPCSpawner**, as illustrated in the next figure.

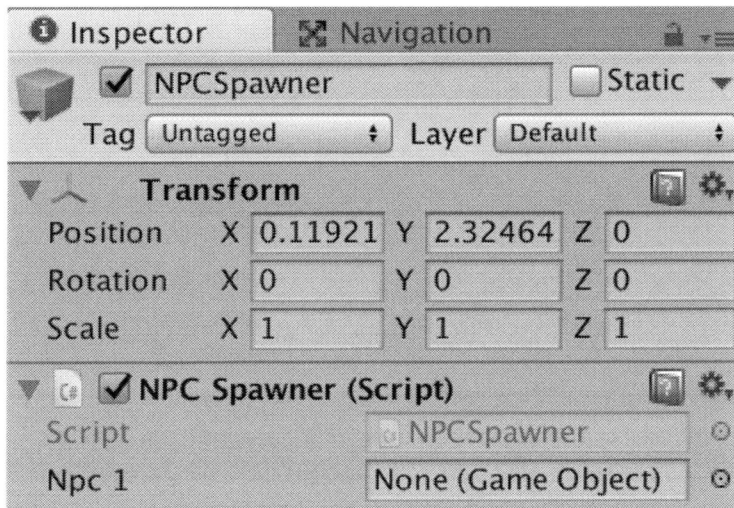

Figure 76: Setting-up the object Spawner (part 1)

- Please drag and drop the prefab **npc1** from the **Project** window, to the field **NPC1**, as illustrated in the next figure.

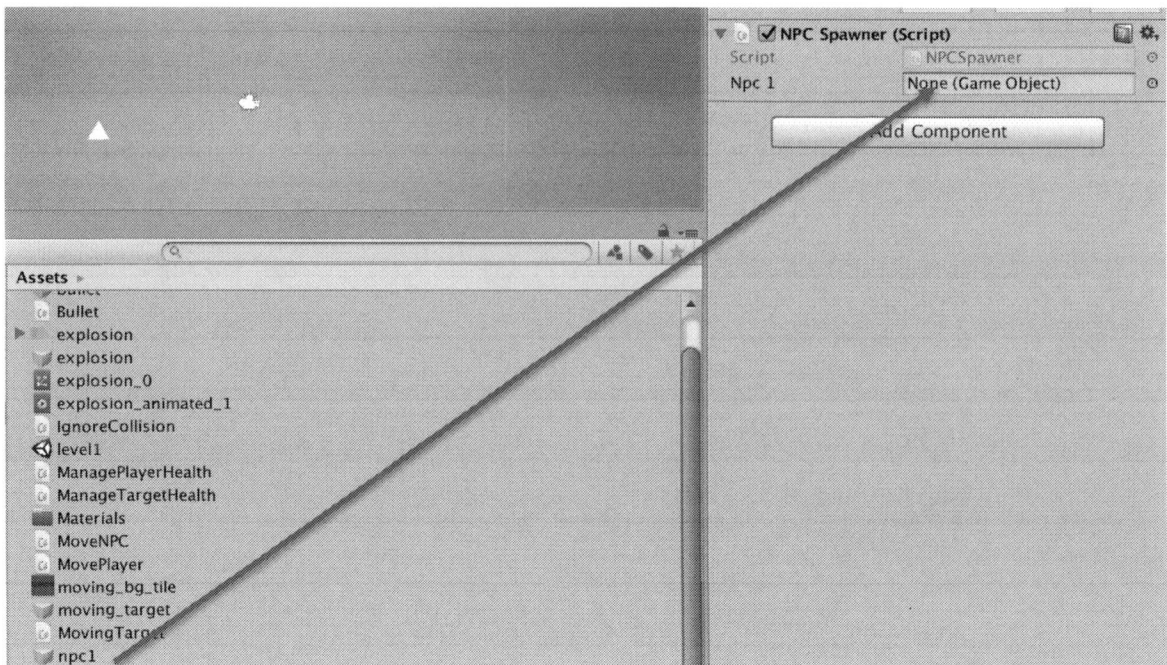

Figure 77: Setting-up the object Spawner (part 2)

- Finally, please move the object **NPCSpawner** close to the top part of the screen, as illustrated on the next figure.

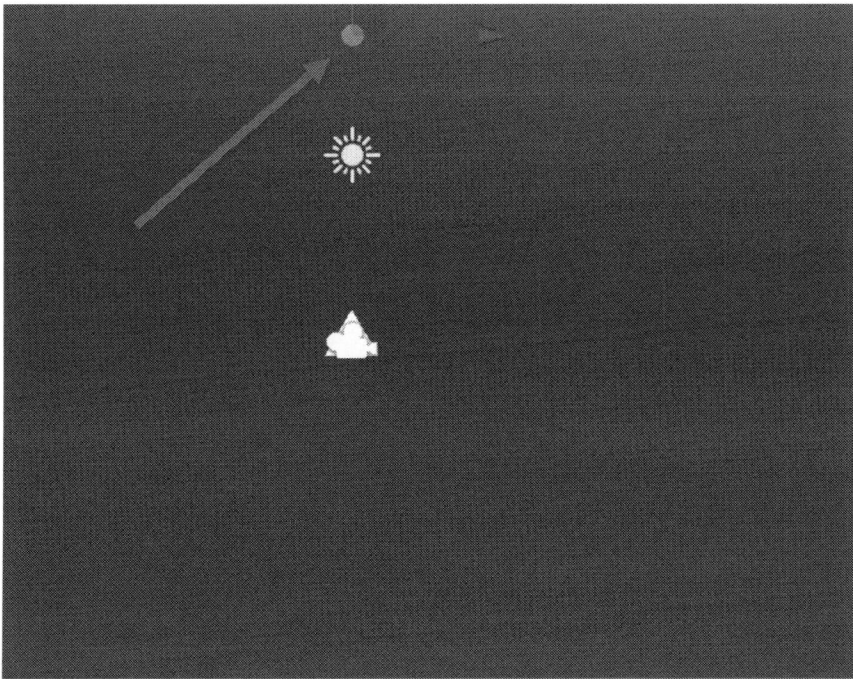

Figure 78: Moving the object NPCSpawner

As you play the scene, you will see that the NPCs are spawn at random positions.

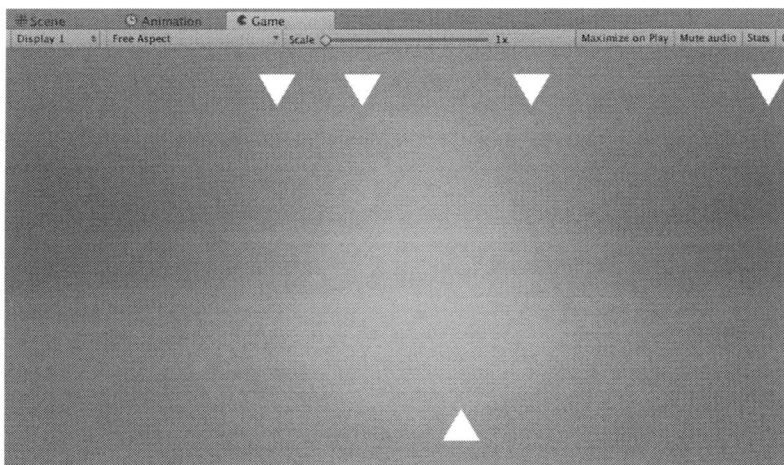

Figure 79: Spawning NPCs

You may notice that the moving targets collide with some of the NPCs; this is because we have previously used a function that ignores collision between two objects (i.e., the object **npc1** and a moving target); however, at this stage we would like to ignore collisions between more than two objects. This is because we now have not just one, but several objects called **npc1**.

So in the next section, we will be using a new technique to ignore collisions between more than two objects; this will involve **layers**. Layers are a way to group objects by adding them to a virtual group called a **layer**; we can then apply specific rules or features to all objects that are included in a specific layer; in our case we will specify that we should be ignoring collisions between objects belonging to two different layers; so, we will do as follows:

- Create a new layer, and add the falling (moving) targets to this layer.

- Create a second new layer, and add each NPC to this new layer.

- Make sure that collisions are ignored between the objects on the first layer and the objects on the second layer.

So let's start!

First we will create a layer for the NPCs and add any NPC based on the prefab **npc1** to this layer:

- Please select the prefab called **npc1** in the **Project** window.

- Then, open the **Inspector** window and locate the section called **Layer**, at the top of the **Inspector** window, as described on the next figure.

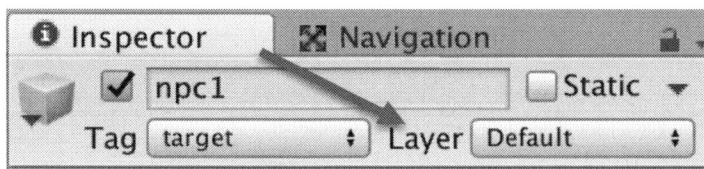

Figure 80: Adding a layer (part 1)

- Click on **Default** (to the right of the label **Layer**); this will display a list of existing layers.

Figure 81: Adding a layer (part 2)

- You can then select the option **Add Layer** from the drop-down menu.

- In the new window, please type the name of the new layer called **NPC** to the right of the label **User Layer 8**.

Figure 82: Adding a layer (part 3)

- Once this is, done, select the prefab **npc1** in the **Project** window.

- Using the **Inspector** window, click on **Default** (to the right of the label **Layer**); this will display a list of existing layers.

- This time, a list that includes your new layer (i.e., **NPC**) should appear; please select the layer called **NPC**.

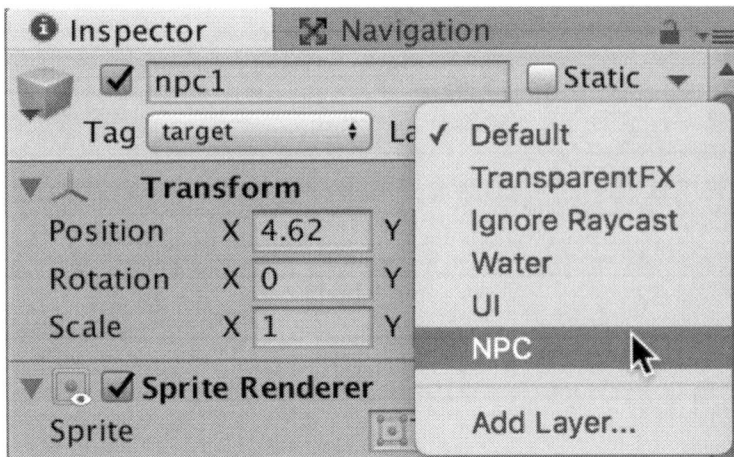

Figure 83: Applying a new layer

So by performing this action, we have specified that each object based on the prefab **npc1** will be on the layer called **NPC**.

Now we just need to specify a layer for the prefab called **moving_target**.

- Please select the prefab called **movingTarget** in the **Project** window.

- Then, open the **Inspector** window and locate the section called **Layer** (as we have done previously), at the top of the **Inspector** window, as described on the next figure.

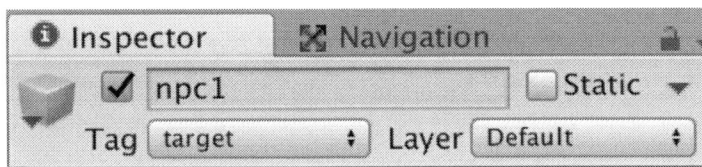

Figure 84: Creating a new layer for moving targets (part 1)

- Click on **Default** (to the right of the label **Layer**); this will display a list of existing layers.

Figure 85: Creating a new layer for moving targets (part 2)

- Select **Add Layer**.

- In the new window, type the name of the new layer called **Target** to the right of the label **User Layer 9**.

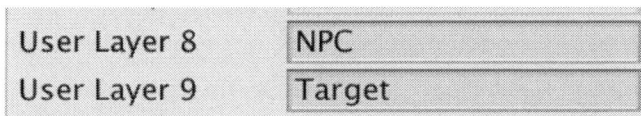

Figure 86: Creating a new layer for moving targets (part 3)

- Once this is, done, please select the prefab **movingTarget** in the **Project** window.

- Using the **Inspector** window, click on the drop-down menu (to the right of the label **Layer**); this will display a list of existing layers.

- This time a list that includes your new layer should appear; please select the layer called **Target**, as illustrated in the next figure.

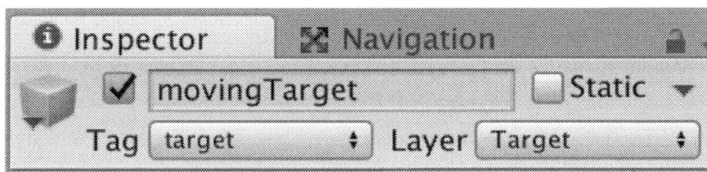

Figure 87:Applying a new layer to the moving targets

- So by performing this action, we have specified that each object based on the prefab **movingTarget** will be on the layer called **Target**.

Last but not least, we need to tell Unity that collisions should be ignored between objects belonging to these two new layers (i.e., objects that belong to the layers called **NPC** and **Target**); this will be done using scripting:

- Please open the script called **IgnoreCollisions**.

- Modify the **Start** function as follows:

```
void Start ()
{
    //if        (GameObject.Find        ("npc1")       !=      null)
Physics2D.IgnoreCollision            (GetComponent<BoxCollider2D>(),
GameObject.Find ("npc1").GetComponent<PolygonCollider2D> ());
    int layer1 = GameObject.Find ("npc1").layer;
    int layer2 = gameObject.layer;
    Physics2D.IgnoreLayerCollision(layer1, layer2, true);
}
```

In the previous code:

- We comment the first line that was originally used to ignore collisions between the object called **npc1** and the moving targets, since we will now use layers for this purpose.

- We then define the index of the two layers that we have created previously (i.e., **NPC** and **Target**). Note that to obtain the ids of these layers, we refer to objects that have been added to these layers. So to find the id of the layer **Target**, we refer to the layer on which the NPC called **npc1** has been added; the same is done for the moving targets (i.e., the object linked to this script).

- These layer indices are expressed as integers.

- **layer2** is the index of the layer (called **Target**) linked to the object (or prefab) that is attached to this script (i.e., **moving_target**)

- **layer1** is the index of the layer (called **NPC**) linked to the object (or prefab) named **npc1**.

Please save your code, and test the scene; you should see that the moving targets do not collide with the NPCs anymore.

LEVEL ROUNDUP

Summary

In this chapter, we have managed to add some interesting features, including artificial intelligence, applying damage to the player, and keeping the player in the field of view. Finally we also learned about layers and how to use them to ignore collisions between more than two objects.

Checklist

You can consider moving to the next stage if you can do the following:

- Understand how to create and apply layers.

- Understand how to ignore collision through scripting .

- Understand how to convert world coordinates to the camera viewport's coordinates.

Quiz

Now, let's check your knowledge! Please answer the following questions (the answers are included in the resource pack) or specify whether they are correct or incorrect.

1. Coordinates in the viewport range from 1 to 100.

2. The following code will convert world coordinates to viewport coordinates:

```
Camera.main.WorldToViewportPoint
```

3. Assuming that npc1 is on a layer called NPC, the following code will return the id of the layer called NPC.

```
int layer1 = GameObject.Find ("npc1").layer;
```

4. The following code will ignore collisions between objects belonging to the first layer and objects belonging to the second layer.

```
Physics2D.IgnoreLayerCollision(layer1, layer2, false);
```

5. By default, all new objects in Unity are allocated the layer called **Unity-Default**.

6. An object can be allocated to several layers.

7. The following code will create a variable that ranges from -10 to +10.

```
float range = Random.Range (-10, 10)
```

8. A polygon collider can be added to an object using the menu **Components | Polygon | PolygonCollider2D**.

9. For a particular script, the function **Start** is called when the script is loaded.

10. For a particular script, the function **Start** is called only when the game is loaded.

Challenge 1

For this chapter, your challenge will be to modify the attributes of the game to make it more or less challenging:

- Modify the frequency at which the NPCs are spawn.
- Modify the speed at which the player moves.

4
POLISHING-UP THE GAME

In this section, we will polish-up our game by adding a few features that will increase the game play, as well as the game flow; after completing this chapter, you will be able to:

- Improve AI by respawning NPCs given that specific conditions are fulfilled.

- Increase the difficulty of your game over time.

- Add a temporary shield to the player.

- Add sound effects.

IMPROVING AI

In this section, we will improve the AI in several ways:

- NPCs will be spawned after 5 seconds.

- The difficulty of the game will increase with time; as time elapses, the NPCs will be spawned more frequently and the falling targets will be generated more frequently also.

So let's get started:

- Please create a new empty object and call it **gameManager**.

- Create a new C# script and rename it **ManageShooterGame**.

- Open this script and modify it as follows.

- Add the following code at the beginning of the class (new code in bold).

```
public class ManageShooterGame : MonoBehaviour {
    public float timer;
    public float difficulty;
    public float timerThresold;
```

- In the previous code, we declare three variables that will be used to increase the difficulty of the game after a specific threshold has been reached by the timer.

- Add the following code in the **Start** function.

```
void Start ()
{
    timer = 0;
    difficulty = 1;
    timerThresold = 5;//difficulty increases after 5 seconds
}
```

- In the previous code: we initialize the time and set the initial **difficulty** level to **1**; the threshold is set to **5**, which means that the difficulty will increase every 5 seconds.

- Please add the following code in the **Update** function.

```
void Update ()
{
    timer += Time.deltaTime;
    if (timer >= timerThresold)
    {
        difficulty++;
        print ("Difficulty level: " + difficulty);
        timer = 0;
    }
}
```

- In the previous code, we update the variable **timer**, so that the difficulty level is increased every time the threshold (i.e., 5 seconds for now) has been reached. The difficulty level is also displayed in the **Console** window, for testing purposes.

- Please save this script (i.e., **manageShooterGame**), check that it is error-free, and then drag and drop it on the objet called **gameManager** in the **Hierarchy** window.

Now we just need to use this difficulty level for the scripts that spawn the moving targets or the NPCs. The idea is that the frequency at which these are spawn will be based on the difficulty level; the higher the difficult level, and the more frequently these objects will be spawn.

So let's modify these scripts:

- Please open the script called **SpawnMovingTarget**, and modify its **Update** function as follows (new code in bold).

```
timer += Time.deltaTime;
float range = Random.Range (-10, 10);//Screen.width);
Vector3          newPosition          =          new          Vector3
(GameObject.Find("player").transform.position.x     +     range,
transform.position.y, 0);
//if (timer >= 1 )
float                    respawnTime                    =
5/GameObject.Find("gameManager").GetComponent<ManageShooterGame>(
).difficulty;
if (timer >= respawnTime)
{
```

In the previous code:

- We create a variable **respawnTime** that is calculated based on the difficulty level; so at the start, **respawnTime** will be 5 and then 2.5, etc; so objects will be respawn twice as fast every time the level of difficulty increases by one; this will make the game extremely challenging over time.

- We then use this **respawnTime** variable to know when the prefab should be instantiated.

You can now save your script, and we can then perform similar modifications for the NPCs.

- Please open the script **NPCSpawner**, and modify its **Update** function as follows (new code in bold).

```
//if (timer >= 1 )
float                          respawnTime                          =
5/GameObject.Find("gameManager").GetComponent<ManageShooterGame>(
).difficulty;
if (timer >= respawnTime)
{
```

- This code is identical to the one we have used to respawn the moving targets.

- You can now save your code.

Note that you can modify the variable **respawnTime** by multiplying it by a number of your choice. As it is, the game will quickly become very challenging as the spawning frequency is doubled every 5 seconds.

ADDING A TEMPORARY SHIELD TO THE PLAYER

While the player can shoot projectiles, given the frequency at which the NPCs are spawn, it would be great for the player to avail of a shield, even temporarily.

So, in this section, we will create a feature whereby:

- A bonus object will be instantiated randomly.

- After collecting this bonus, the player will avail of a shield and be invincible for 5 seconds.

- While it is invincible, a blue circle will be displayed around the player.

This will involve the following:

- Creating a tag for the bonus.

- Detecting collision with this bonus based on its tag.

- Creating a shield, based on a sprite.

- Initially deactivate the shield (i.e., make it invisible).

- Creating a timer to determine for how long the shield should be active.

- Activate the shield (i.e., make it visible) after the bonus has been collected, and ignore collisions with bullets or targets while the shield is active.

- Deactivate the shield when the timer has reached 5 seconds.

So let's implement this feature:

- Please create a new sprite: from the **Project** window, select **Create | Sprites | Circle**.

- Rename this asset **shield**.

Figure 88: Creating a new shield

- Drag and drop this asset (i.e., the shield) to the **Scene** view; this will create a new object called **shield**.

- Using the **Hierarchy**, drag and drop this object (i.e., the shield) on top of the object called **player**, so that it becomes a child of the object **player**, as illustrated on the next figure.

▼ player
    shield

Figure 89: Adding the shield as a child of the object player

- Once this is done, you can click on the object called **shield** in the **Hierarchy**, and then look at the **Inspector** window.

- In the **Inspector** window, set the position of this object (i.e., the shield) to **(0, 0, 0)** and its scale attributes to **(1, 1, 1)**.

You can also change the color and transparency of the sprite for this object as follows:

- Using the **Inspector**, for the **Component** called **Sprite Renderer**, click on the white rectangle to the right of the attribute called **Color**.

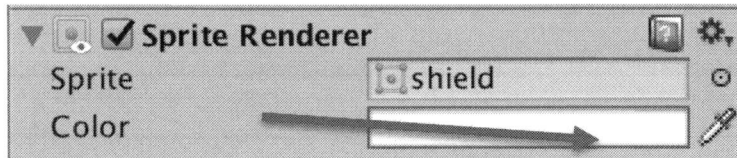

▼ ✔ **Sprite Renderer**

Sprite   shield

Color

Figure 90: Changing the color of the shield

- This will open a new window; using this window you can pick a blue color of your choice, and also set the **opacity** to **70**, as illustrated on the next figures.

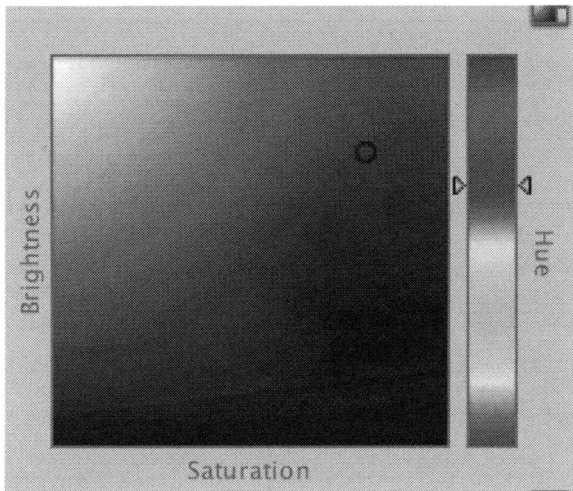

Figure 91: Painting the shield in blue

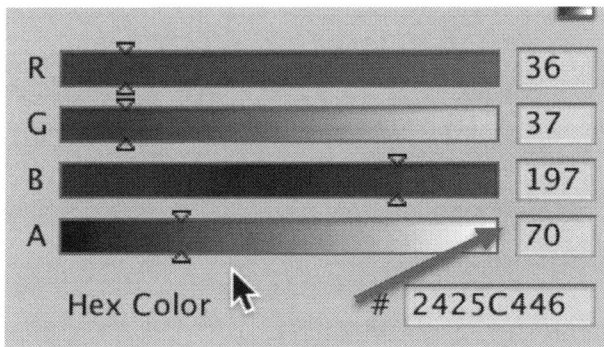

Figure 92: Setting the opacity to 70

- Once this is done, the player should look like the following figure:

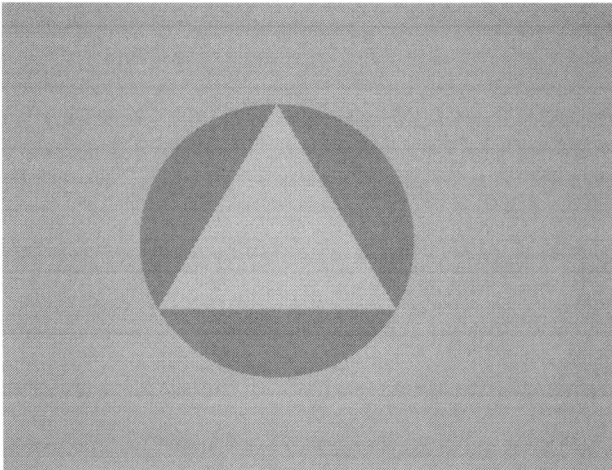

Figure 93: The player and its shield

Next, we will create a prefab that will be used as a bonus to be collected by the player to activate its shield.

- In the **Project** window, please duplicate the prefab called **movingTarget** (i.e., select the prefab and then press **CTRL + D**).

- Rename the duplicate **bonus**.

Figure 94: Creating a new prefab for the bonus

- Once this is done, please click on the prefab called **bonus** that you have just created in the **Project** window, so that we can modify some of its properties.

- Using the **Inspector** window, create a new tag called **bonus** and apply it to this object, as we have done previously for other objects.

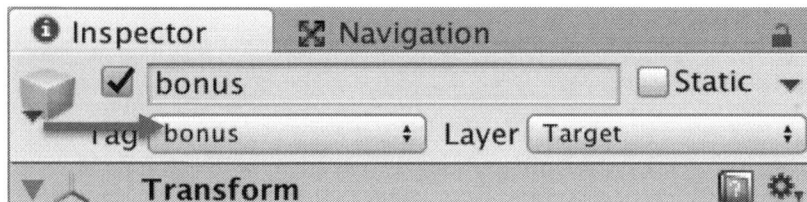

Figure 95: Adding a tag to the bonus prefab

- Please change the color of the sprite for this prefab to green using its **Sprite Renderer** component in the **Inspector**.

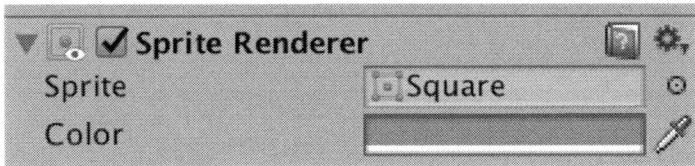

Figure 96: Changing the color of the bonus

So, this new prefab will behave the same way as the moving platforms, in the sense that, once spawned, it will move downwards; however, this **bonus** prefab has a different tag called **bonus**, so that he player can collect it; the **bonus** prefab also has a distinctive color (i.e., green) so that the player can tell it apart from the falling targets.

So now that we have created this prefab, we will need to spawn it and to ensure that when it is collected by the player, that the player's shield is activated accordingly.

So we will need to modify a few of the existing scripts: the script that spawns moving targets, and the other script that manages the player's health.

- Please open the script **SpawnMovingTargets**.

- Add the following code at the beginning of the class (new code in bold).

```
public GameObject newObject;
public GameObject bonus;
```

- Modify the function **Update** as follows (new code in bold).

```
if (timer >= respawnTime)
{
    float typeOfObjectSpwan = Random.Range(0,100);
    GameObject t;
    if (typeOfObjectSpwan >= 50)
    {
        t = (GameObject)(Instantiate (newObject, newPosition,
Quaternion.identity));
        t.GetComponent<ManageTargetHealth>      ().type      =
ManageTargetHealth.TARGET_BOULDER;
    }
    else t = (GameObject)(Instantiate (bonus, newPosition,
Quaternion.identity));
    //GameObject t = (GameObject)(Instantiate (newObject,
newPosition, Quaternion.identity));
    //t.GetComponent<ManageTargetHealth>      ().type      =
ManageTargetHealth.TARGET_BOULDER;
    timer = 0;
}
```

In the previous code:

- We generate a random number between 0 and 100; this number will be used to determine what object should be spawn; here, we are effectively specifying a probability of 50% chance for bonuses to be spawn and a 50% chance for moving targets to be spawn. This is a very simple way to apply probabilities (and random behaviors) to your games.

- If the random number id **50 or more**, we instantiate a moving target. Otherwise, we instantiate a bonus.

Note that **Random.Range** will generate numbers from a range that includes the boundaries of this range; in our case the number generated will range between 0 and 100 inclusive, which would include 101 possibilities; so to be more accurate, we could adjust the upper boundary of the range to 99, which would result in 100 possibilities.

- The previous code used to instantiate a moving target is commented.

That's it!

Please save your script and check that it is error-free.

Next, we can modify the script that manages the player's health.

- Please open the script **ManagePlayerHealth**.

- Modify the beginning of the class as follows:

```
public float timerForShield;
public bool startInvincibility;
void Start ()
{
    GameObject.Find        ("shield").GetComponent<SpriteRenderer>
().enabled = false;


}
```

In the previous code:

- We declare two variables: **timerForShield** and **startInvincibility**.

- We also make sure that the shield is not displayed at the start of the game by **not** rendering the corresponding sprite.

We can now modify the collision detection to account for the shield (and the temporary invincibility).

- Please modify the function **OnCollisionEnter2D**, in the script **ManagePlayerHealth**, as follows (new code in bold):

```
if ((coll.gameObject.tag == "target" || coll.gameObject.tag ==
"bullet") && !startInvincibility)
{
    Destroy (coll.gameObject);

    DestroyPlayer ();
}

if (coll.gameObject.tag == "bonus")
{
    Destroy (coll.gameObject);
    startInvincibility = true;
    GameObject.Find        ("shield").GetComponent<SpriteRenderer>
().enabled = true;
}
```

In the previous code:

- The player will sustain damage only when it is not invincible (i.e., when the shield is not active).

- We also check that the player has collided with a bonus.

- If this is the case, the bonus is destroyed, the player becomes invincible (for the time-being) and the shield is displayed. The variable **startInvincibility** is used to start a timer that will determine when this invincibility will stop.

Finally, we just need to modify the **Update** function to be able to implement the timer, and to check how long the shield should be active.

- Please modify the **Update** function in the script **ManagePlayerHealth** as follows (new code in bold):

```
void Update ()
{
    if (startInvincibility)
    {
        timerForShield += Time.deltaTime;
        if (timerForShield >= 20)
        {
            timerForShield = 0;
            startInvincibility = false;
            GameObject.Find
("shield").GetComponent<SpriteRenderer> ().enabled = false;
        }
    }
}
```

In the previous code:

- We check whether the player is invincible (i.e., if a bonus shield has been collected).

- If this is the case, the value of the timer is increased every second, until it reaches 20 seconds.

- In this case, the timer is reset to 0, the invincibility is set to **false**, and the shield is no longer displayed onscreen.

Last but not least, we need to add the bonus prefab to the object **targetSpawner**.

- Please select the object **targetSpawner** in the **Hierarchy**.

- Then drag and drop the prefab **bonus** from the **Project** window, to the field called **bonus** for the component called **SpawnMovingTargets**, as described on the next figure.

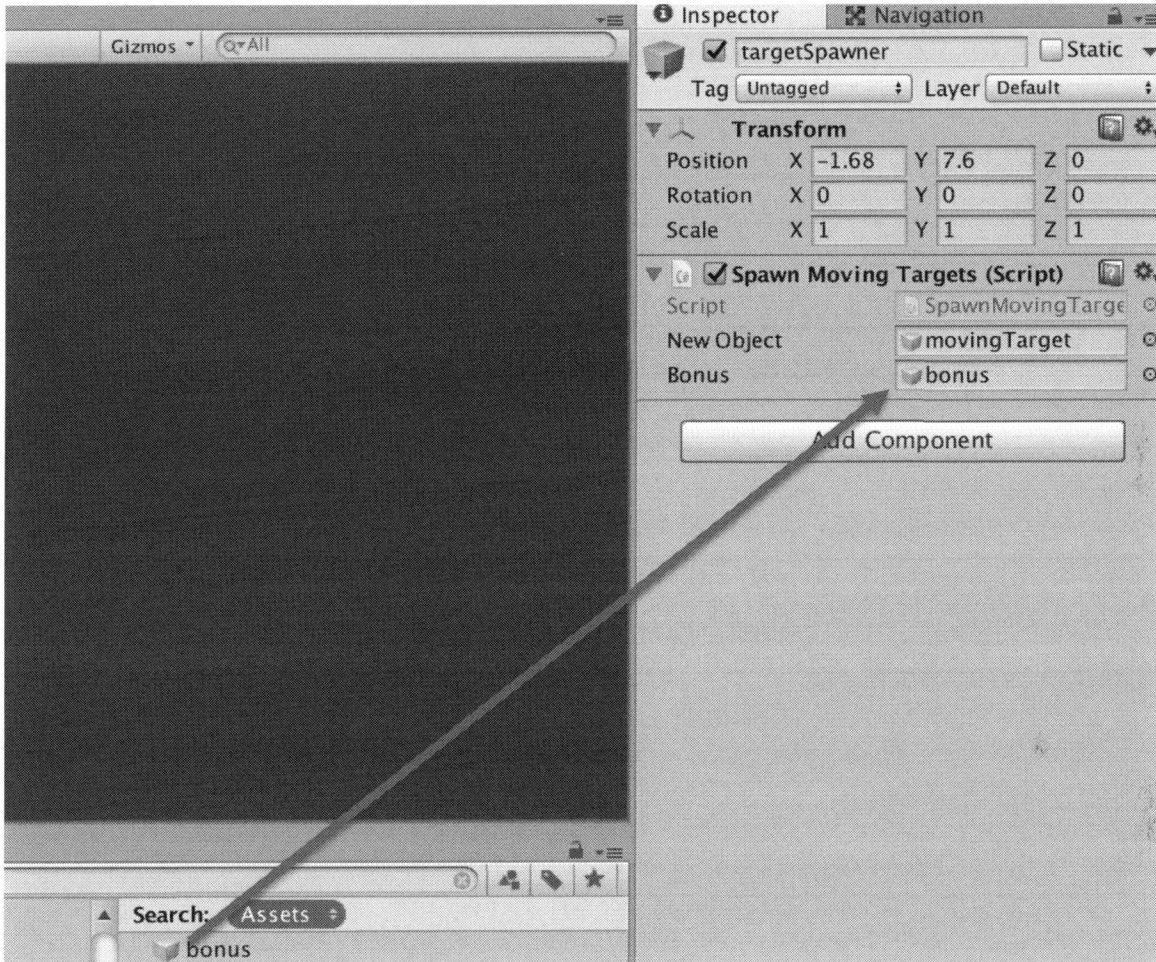

Figure 97: Adding the bonus to the targetSpawner object

Once this is done, you can now test your game: after collecting a bonus, the shield should appear for 20 seconds, allowing you to be invincible for that duration.

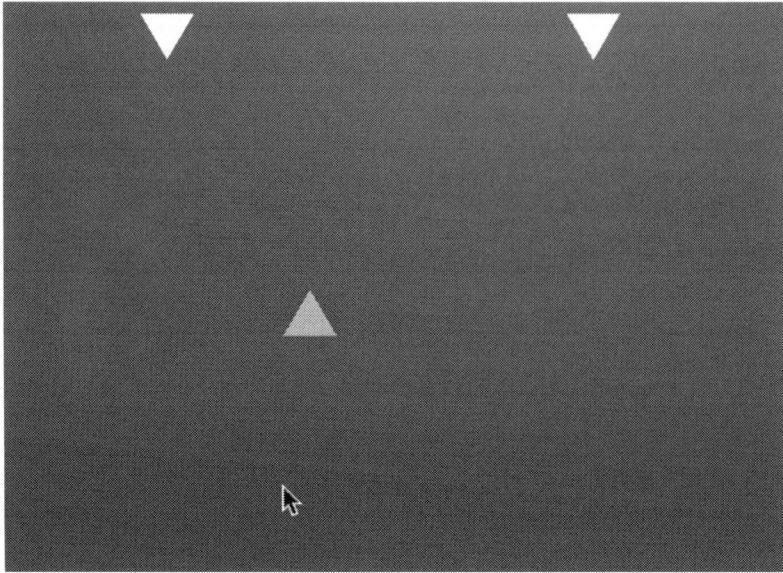

Figure 98: Using the shield

ADDING A SCORE

Now that our gameplay is improved thanks to randomly instantiated NPCs and an increasing difficulty, we could add and display a score. This will consist of a **UI Text** object that will be updated from a script every time the player manages to hit a target.

- Please create a new **UI Text** object; from the main menu, select: **GameObject | UI | Text**. This will create a new object called **Text**, along with a parent object called **Canvas**.

Figure 99: Adding a UI Text object

- To know where this object is in relation to the game screen, you can just double click on it in the **Hierarchy**.

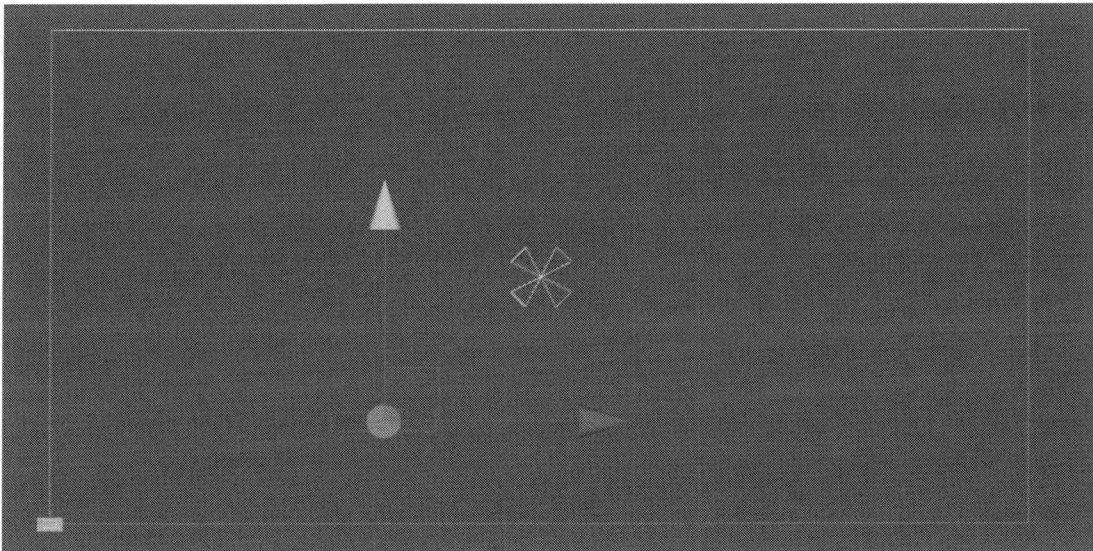

Figure 100: Locating the UI Text object

- Then, in the **Scene** view, move this object, to the top-left corner of the white rectangle that defines the game screen.

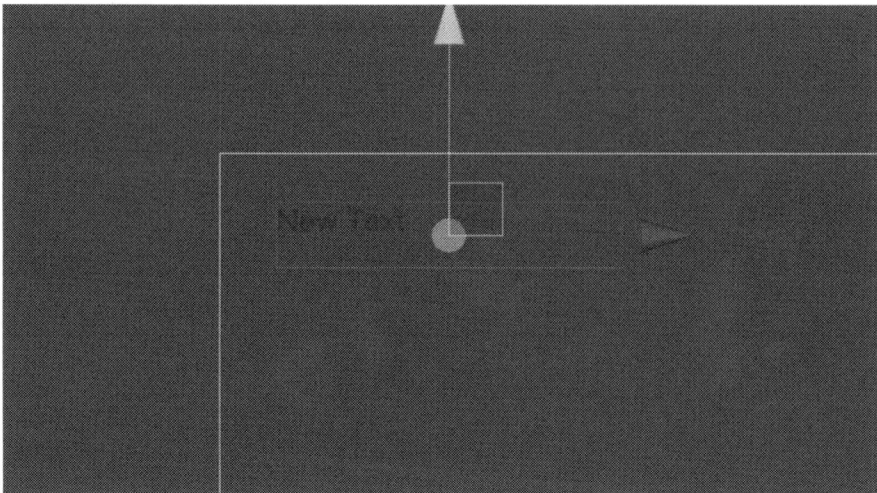

Figure 101: Moving the UI text object

We can now change some of the properties of this object (e.g., color and size):

- After selecting the object called **Text** in the **Hierarchy**, please use the **Inspector** window to change the color of its text to **white** (in the component called **Text**).

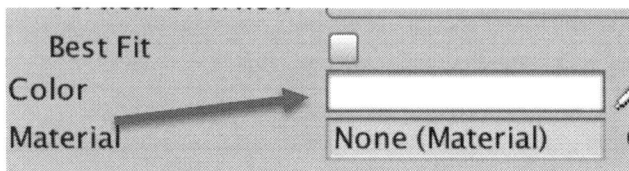

Figure 102: Changing the color of the text

- Please modify its alignment as described in the next figure:

Figure 103: Modifying the alignment of the Text object

- You can also rename this object **uIScrore**, using the **Hierarchy** window.

Once this is done, we just need to calculate the score and display it in the **UI Text** object.

- Please, open the script called **ManagePlayerHealth**.

- Add the following code at the start of the script (new code in bold):

```
using UnityEngine;
using System.Collections;
using UnityEngine.SceneManagement;
using UnityEngine.UI;
```

- Add the following code at the beginning of the class (new code in bold).

```
public float timerForShield;
public bool startInvincibility;
public int score;
void Start ()
{
    score = 0;
    GameObject.Find        ("shield").GetComponent<SpriteRenderer>
().enabled = false;
    GameObject.Find    ("scoreUI").GetComponent<Text>    ().text    =
"Score:" + score;

}
```

In the previous script:

- We declare a new variable called **score**.

- At the beginning of the scene, we set this variable (i.e., **score**) to **0**.

- We also initialize the text displayed by the **UI Text** component.

Please add the following code at the end of the class, just before the last closing curly bracket.

```
public void increaseScore()
{
    score++;
    GameObject.Find    ("scoreUI").GetComponent<Text>    ().text    =
"Score:" + score;
}
```

In the previous script:

- We create a new function called **increaseScore**.

- In this function, we increase the **score** by **1**.

- We also update the **UI Text** object to reflect the change in the **score**.

Please save this script, and check that it is error-free.

The next thing we need to do is to call this function when the bullet fired by the player has hit a target; this will be managed in the script called **Bullet**.

Note that the function **increaseScore** is public, which means that it will be accessible from outside its class, and as a result, from the script called **Bullet**.

So let's modify the script called **Bullet**:

- Please open the script called **Bullet**.

- Add the following code to the function **OnCollisionEnter2D** (new code in bold).

```
coll.gameObject.GetComponent<ManageTargetHealth>().gotHit(10);
GameObject.Find      ("player").GetComponent<ManagePlayerHealth>
().increaseScore ();
Destroy (gameObject);
```

- Please save your code.

You can now check the game to see whether the score is displayed and updated accordingly as your bullets hit different targets.

ADDING AUDIO

The last thing we will do is to add audio to our game whenever the player is hit, or s/he fires bullets. For this purpose, we will import two sound effects, and play them accordingly.

Please import the audio files **explosion.wav** and **bullet.wav** from the resource pack to Unity's **Project** window.

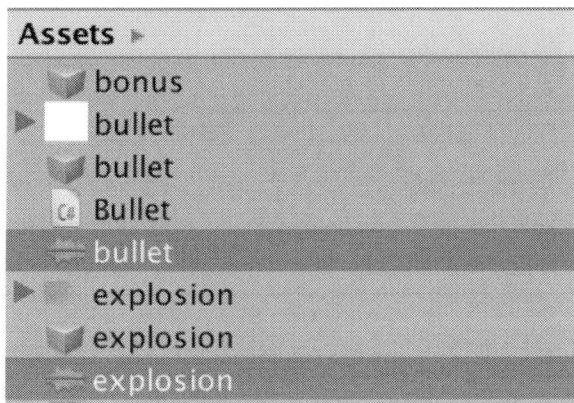

Figure 104: Importing audio

The two audio files were created using the site http://www.bfxr.net/, which is a free tool to create your own sound effects.

Next, we will create the necessary components to be able to play these sounds, and we will start with the sound for the bullet.

- Please select the object called **player** in the **Hierarchy**.

- From the top menu, select **Component | Audio | Audio Source**; this will add an **Audio Source** component to your object.

Whenever you need to play a sound, an **Audio Source** is needed, and it is comparable to an mp3 player in the sense that it plays audio clips that you need to select, the same way you would select a particular track on your mp3 player.

- Please, drag and drop the audio file called **bullet** from the **Project** window to the **Audio Clip** attribute of the **Audio Source**.

Figure 105: Adding an audio source

- You can then set the attribute **Play on Awake** to **false** (i.e., unchecked) so that this sound is not played automatically at the start of the scene, as illustrated on the next figure.

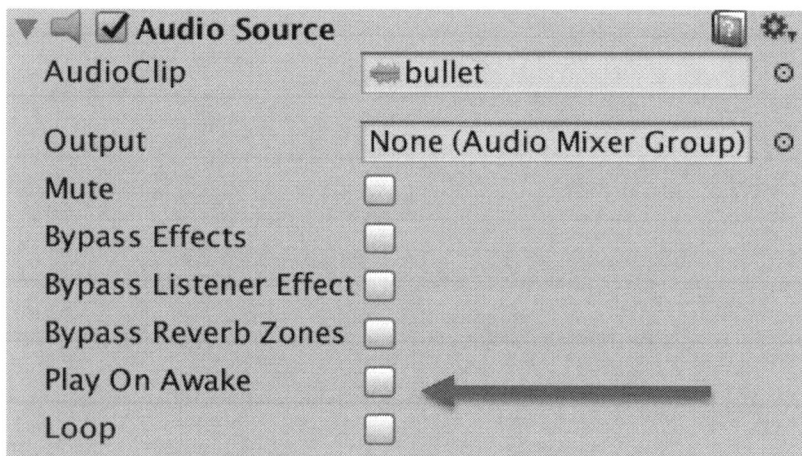

Figure 106: Setting the attributes of the sound effect

Next, we will write code that will access this **Audio Source** and play the clip, whenever the player fires a bullet.

- Please open the script called **MovePlayer**.

- Add the following code to the function **Update** (new cold in bold).

```
if (Input.GetKeyDown (KeyCode.Space))
{
    GameObject   b   =   (GameObject)(Instantiate   (bullet,
transform.position + transform.up*1.5f, Quaternion.identity));
    b.GetComponent<Rigidbody2D>   ().AddForce   (transform.up   *
1000);
    GetComponent<AudioSource> ().Play ();
}
```

In the previous code, we access the **AudioSource** component that is linked to the object **player** (i.e., the object linked to this script), and we play the clip that is included in this **AudioSource** (i.e., **bullet**).

Please save your code, test the scene, and check that the audio clip is played whenever you press the space bar.

Next, using the same principle, we will generate the sound of an explosion when the player is hit.

Now, because the **Audio Source** will need to play several sounds (a different sound depending on whether the player fires a bullet or is hit), we will need to specify which track needs to be played, so we will modify our script accordingly.

- Please open the script **MovePlayer**.

- Add the following line at the beginning of the script:

```
public AudioClip fireSound;
```

- This code declares an audio clip; because it is public, it will be accessible from the **Inspector**, and as a result, we will be able to set (or initialize) this variable by dragging and dropping objects to its placeholders in the **Inspector** window.

- Please save your script, switch to Unity, select the **player** object and display the **Inspector** window.

- You should see that a variable called **fireSound**, that acts as placeholder, is now available in the component called **Move**.

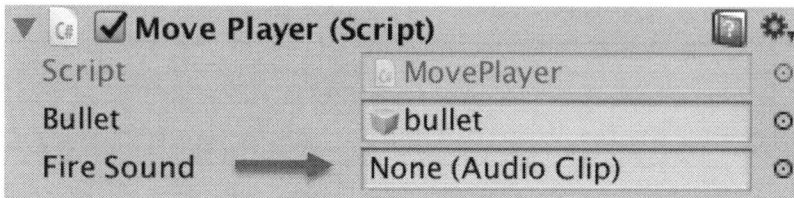

Figure 107: Initializing the audio clips (part1)

- Please drag and drop the sound **bullet.wav** from the **Project** view, to the variable **fireSound** in the **Inspector**, as illustrated in the next figure.

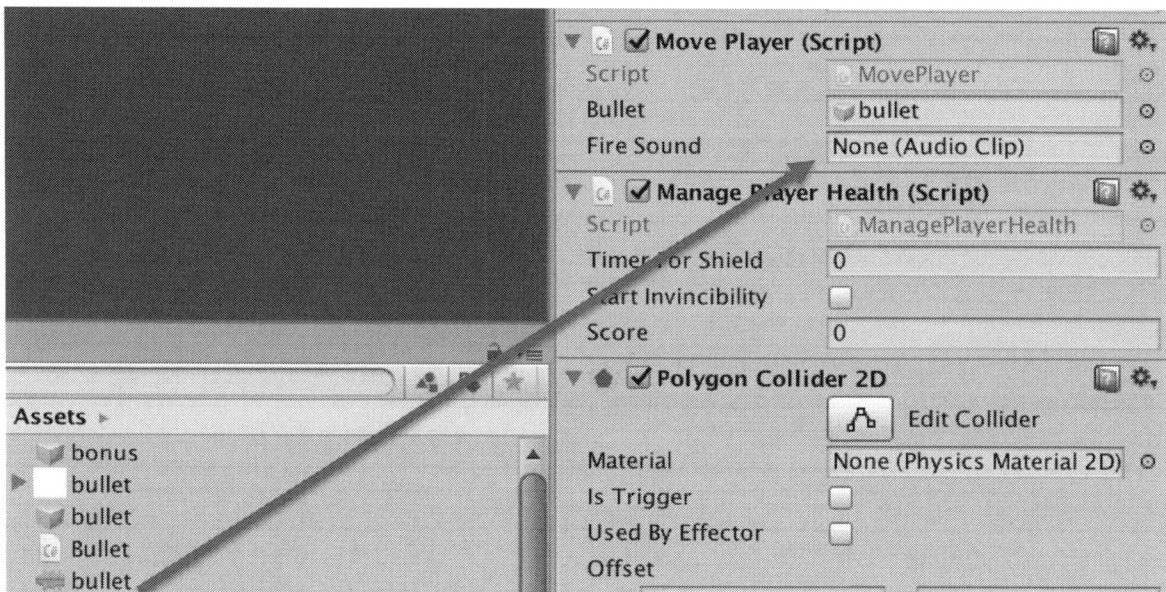

Figure 108: Initializing the audio clips (part 2)

Now, it's time to modify the script further to tell the system which audio clip to play and when.

- Please open the script **MovePlayer**.

- Add the following code to the **Update** function (new code in bold):

```
if (Input.GetKeyDown (KeyCode.Space))
{
    GameObject    b    =    (GameObject)(Instantiate    (bullet,
transform.position + transform.up*1.5f, Quaternion.identity));
    b.GetComponent<Rigidbody2D>    ().AddForce    (transform.up    *
1000);
    GetComponent<AudioSource> ().clip = fireSound;
    GetComponent<AudioSource> ().Play ();
}
```

In the previous code:

- We specify that we should play the clip called **fireSound** (which contains the audio **bullet.wav**); this track is now the default (or active) track for the **Audio Source**.

- We then play the track that we have selected.

Next, we will use a similar technique to play a different sound when the player is hurt.

- Please open the script called **ManagePlayerHealth**.

- Add the following lines at the beginning of the script:

```
public AudioClip hitSound;
```

- This code declares an audio clip; because it is public, it will be accessible from the **Inspector**, and as a result, we will be able to set (or initialize) this variable by dragging and dropping objects to its placeholders in the **Inspector** window.

- Add the following code to the function **DestroyPlayer** (new code in bold).

```
void DestroyPlayer()
{
    GetComponent<AudioSource> ().clip = hitSound;
    GetComponent<AudioSource> ().Play ();
    SceneManager.LoadScene (SceneManager.GetActiveScene().name);
}
```

Once this is done, we just need to initialize the variable **hitSound** from the **Inspector** window.

- Please save your script, switch to Unity, select the **player** object and display the **Inspector** window.

[129]

- You should see that a variable called **hitSound**, for the component **ManagePlayerHealth**, that acts as placeholder, is now available.

Figure 109: Initializing the audio clips (part1)

- Please drag and drop the sound **explosion.wav** from the **Project** view, to the variable **hitSound** in the **Inspector**, as illustrated in the next figure.

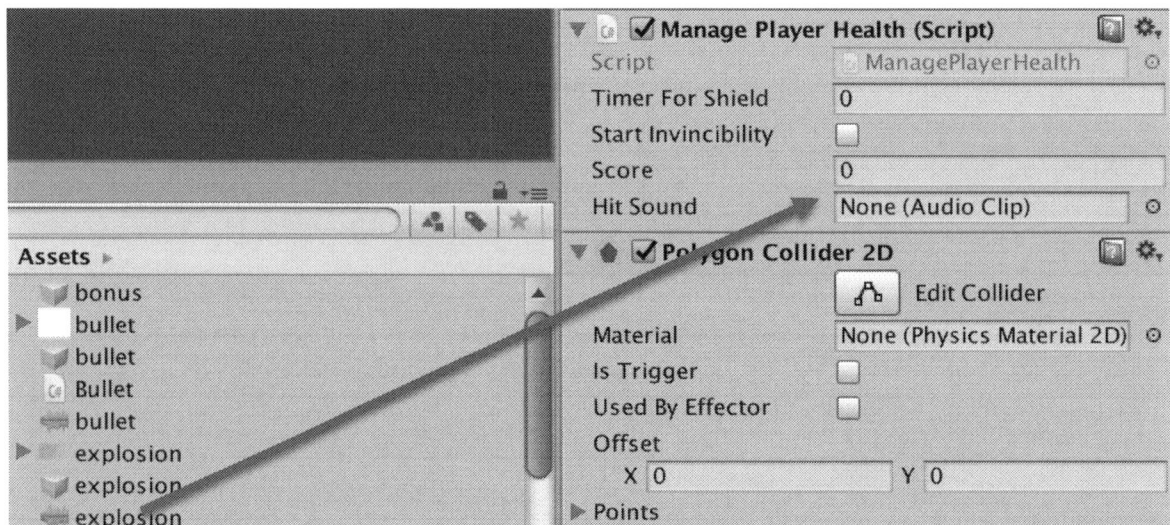

Figure 110: Initializing the audio clips (part 2)

You can now test your scene: when the player is hit, the explosion sound should be played.

5
FREQUENTLY ASKED QUESTIONS

This chapter provides answers to the most frequently asked questions about the features that we have covered in this book. Please also note that some <u>videos are also available on the companion site</u> to help you with some of the concepts covered in this book.

USER INTERACTION

How can I detect keystrokes?

You can detect keystroke by using the function **Input.GetKey**. For example, the following code detects when the key E is pressed; this code should be added to the **Update** function.

```
If (Input.GetKey(KeyCode.E)){}
```

How can I play sound?

To play a sound, you need to add an **Audio Source** component to an object; when this is done, you can either play its default audio clip, or select which audio clip should be played.

```
GetComponent<AudioSource>().Play();//plays the default sound
GetComponent<AudioSource>().clip = clip1;//selects the clip
GetComponent<AudioSource>().Play();//plays clip selected
```

How can I display text onscreen?

To display text onscreen you will need to create a **UI Text** object, and then access it through a script. For example:

```
GetComponent<Text>().text = "New Text";
```

FIRING OBJECTS

How can I ensure that a projectile will not be subject to gravity?

If a projectile includes a Rigidbody2D component, you can make sure that it is not subject to gravity by setting its **gravity scale** attribute to 0.

How can I set a projectile in movement?

To set a projectile in movement, you need to apply a force to it. For example, to move it up the screen, the following code could be used.

```
GetComponent<Rigidbody2D> ().AddForce (transform.up * 1000);
```

Improving Gameplay

How can I create random numbers?

You can use the function called **Random.Range** to create a random number; for example, the following code will create a number between -10 and +10.

```
Random.Range (-10, 10)
```

How can I make some attributes temporary (e.g., invincibility)?

You can use a timer that can determine from when and for how long a variable should have a specific value; the timer can start at 0 and then increase until it has reached a specific threshold; when this is the case, a new value can be set for the variable. The following code snippet illustrates how this can be done.

```
void Update()
{
      timer+=Time.deltaTime;
      float threshold = 5.0f;
      if (timer > thresold)
      {
      ...
      }
{
```

6
THANK YOU

I would like to thank you for completing this book; I trust that you are now comfortable with creating a simple 2D shooter game. This book is the second in the series "A Beginner's Guide to" that will cover particular aspects of Unity, so it may be time to move on to the next books where you will get started with more specific features such as 2D puzzle games or Character Animation. You can find a description of these forthcoming books on the official page http://www.learntocreategames.com/beginners-guide-to-unity/.

In case you have not seen it yet, you can subscribe to our Facebook group using the following link; it includes a community of like-minded game creators who share ideas and are ready to help you with your game projects.

http://facebook.com/groups/learntocreategames/

You may also subscribe to our mailing list to receive weekly updates and information on how to create games and improve your skills.

http://learntocreategames.com/2d-platform-games/

So that the book can be constantly improved, I would really appreciate your feedback. So, please leave me a helpful review on Amazon letting me know what you thought of the book and also send me an email (learntocreategames@gmail.com) with any suggestions you may have. I read and reply to every email.

Thanks so much!!

Printed in Great Britain
by Amazon